The
BEATITUDES

---

*Living the Life
of Christ*

SOPHIA
INSTITUTE
FOR TEACHERS

About Sophia Institute for Teachers

Sophia Institute for Teachers was launched in 2013 by Sophia Institute to renew and rebuild Catholic culture through service to Catholic education. With the goal of nurturing the spiritual, moral, and cultural life of souls, and an abiding respect for the role and work of teachers, we strive to provide materials and programs that are at once enlightening to the mind and ennobling to the heart; faithful and complete, as well as useful and practical. Sophia Institute is a 501(c)(3) non-profit organization founded in 1983.

Printed in the United States of America
Design by Perceptions Design Studio

Beatitudes: Living the Life of Christ
ISBN: 978-1-622823-000

Contents

■ **Elementary**   ■ **Middle School**   ■ **High School**

Unit One: Foundations of Christian Moral Theology

Unit Two: Living the Life of Christ

Acknowledgments

EDITOR

Veronica Burchard
Sophia Institute for Teachers

CONTRIBUTING WRITER

Elisabeth Rochon
Sophia Institute for Teachers

DESIGN

Carolyn McKinney
Perceptions Studio, Amherst, NH

ACADEMIC ADVISORS

Douglas G. Bushman, S.T.L.
Augustine Institute

Monsignor John Cihak
Pontifical Gregorian University

TEACHER AUTHORS

Sarah Brenner
St. Francis of Assisi Catholic School
Wichita, KS

Sarah is a catechist and primary school teacher in the Diocese of Wichita, Kansas, where she was awarded the St. Rose Philippine Duchesne Award for teachers in 2015. She assists with her parish RCIC program, leads faculty book and bible studies, and serves on various committees. She has a deep love for children and sharing the Faith with them. In her free time, she enjoys studying the lives of the saints, methods of catechesis, and the Catholic spiritual tradition.

Sean Fitzpatrick
Gregory the Great Academy
Scranton, PA

Sean is a graduate of Thomas Aquinas College and taught for 10 years at a Catholic liberal arts boarding school for boys in Elmhurst, Pennsylvania. In 2012 he helped found Gregory the Great Academy, a boarding school for boys in the classical, Catholic tradition, where he serves as headmaster. Sean has also done work as an illustrator, writer, folk musician, and wood carver. He lives in Scranton, Pennsylvania, with his wife and five children.

Jose Gonzalez
Director of Professional Development
Sophia Institute for Teachers

Before joining Sophia Institute for Teachers as Director of Professional Development, Jose worked as a high school teacher and co-department chair at Bishop Carroll Catholic High School in Wichita, Kansas for 10 years. He has worked as a Youth Minister and a Coordinator of *Totus Tuus* in the Archdiocese of Denver. Jose is an experienced speaker at youth and confirmation retreats, Theology on Tap, RCIA classes, and adult faith formation.

Jose has his B.A. in Theology with a concentration in Religious Education from Franciscan University of Steubenville, and his M.A. in evangelization and catechesis from the Augustine Institute.

Mike Gutzwiller

St. Thomas More High School
Milwaukee, WI

Mike is the chair of the theology department at St. Thomas More High School in Milwaukee, Wisconsin, where he has taught for the past 6 years. Mike studied theology and catechetics at Franciscan University of Steubenville and earned a master's degree from Marquette University in school counseling. He is currently studying educational policy and leadership at Marquette University. Mike is also the coordinator of music and sound for Arise Missions and the keyboardist for the Arise worship band. When not teaching, studying, or spending time with his beautiful wife, Sarah, Mike can be found reading one of his nearly 10,000 comic books or working on his latest work of art.

Mark Lajoie

Bishop Guertin High School
Nashua, NH

Mark has a master's degree in Theology from Assumption College, and has been teaching religion for close to 15 years at Bishop Guertin High School in Nashua, New Hampshire. In addition to the joy he finds teaching, he is also an award-winning lead singer, composer, and guitarist at Living Waters Music, a music ministry.

Michael McLaughlin

Saint Benedict Academy
Manchester, NH

Michael attended Catholic schools since pre-K. He received a B.A. in history from the College of the Holy Cross and his M.Ed. and Master's in administration from the University of Notre Dame. Michael taught for seven years at Saint Patrick Catholic High School in Biloxi, Mississippi, and is currently the principal of Saint Benedict Academy in Manchester, New Hampshire.

Steven Jonathan Rummelsburg

Holy Spirit Preparatory Academy
Atlanta, GA

Steven is a Catholic convert, a catechist, a Catholic writer and speaker on matters of Faith, culture, and education. He holds a degree in history from the University of California, Santa Barbara. Steven is a senior contributor at *The Imaginative Conservative*, a regular contributor to the *Integrated Catholic Life*, a contributor to *The Civilized Reader*, *The Standard Bearers*, and *Catholic Exchange*. Steven teaches theology, philosophy, and Church history at Holy Spirit Prep in Atlanta, Georgia.

Derek Tremblay

Mount Royal Academy
Sunapee, NH

Derek is the headmaster at Mount Royal Academy in Sunapee, New Hampshire. Before serving as headmaster, he taught theology classes to grades 7-12 for 5 years. He received a B.A. in theology and political science (08), as well as M.A. in theological studies (09) from Providence College. Derek lives in Goshen, New Hampshire, with his wife and two young children.

Michael Verlander
Holy Spirit Preparatory Academy
Atlanta, GA

A native of Atlanta, GA, Mike holds a B.A. in Philosophy from the Thomas More College of Liberal Arts in Merrimack, NH, and an M.T.S. from Holy Spirit College. He is in his twelfth year of teaching at Holy Spirit Preparatory School, where he chairs the theology department. He also teaches philosophy at Holy Spirit College. In catechesis, he has experience teaching all student levels including adult education at several parishes. Along with attending academic and teaching seminars in liberal and Catholic education, a cherished highlight of his career is leading trips to Rome, Italy, for each year for the last 10 years. He and his wife, Linda, reside in Newnan, Georgia, where they raise their five children: Mary, Thomas, Veronica, John, and Francis.

Janet Wigoff
Pope John Paul II High School
Royersford, PA

Janet is the theology department chairperson at Pope John Paul II High School. She also serves as the secondary theology curriculum committee chairperson for the seventeen high schools in the Archdiocese of Philadelphia. She has a passionate commitment to Jewish-Catholic interfaith dialogue through the Friends in Faith program for students and Bearing Witness for educators. Janet has written six secondary theology modules for Castle Learning, a multi-discipline, on-line learning resource for students. Ave Maria Press has published her mini-unit on Religious Liberty. Her M.A. in theology from St. Charles Borromeo Seminary and her M.B.A in computer sciences from Temple University are treasured foundations.

SPECIAL THANKS TO OUR FIELD-TESTING TEACHERS

Jacqueline Brown
Sacred Heart School
Hampton, NH

Kristina Boufford
St. Casimir School
Manchester, NH

Teresa Chu
Nativity Catholic School
El Monte, CA

Kelly Clifford
St. Catherine of Siena School
Manchester, NH

Trisha Duman
St. Joseph School
Salem, OR

Darleen F. Farland
Cathedral High School
Springfield, MA

Claire M. Griffin
Sacred Heart Academy
(1985-2002)
Honolulu, HI

Jennifer Haile
Cathedral School
Natchez, MS

Joseph Inverso
La Purisima Concepcion
Catholic School
Lompoc, CA

Kathleen Johnston
St. Benedict Academy
Manchester, NH

Elizabeth M. La Dou
Nativity Catholic School
El Monte, CA

Kristen Law
Homeschooling Parent
Colorado Springs, CO

Kenneth Monreal
Blessed Sacrament School
Hollywood, CA

Christina O'Brien
St. Elizabeth Seton School
Rochester, NH

Deacon Sergio Perez
Holy Angels School
Arcadia, CA

Regina Rebovich
Academy of St. Dorothy
Staten Island, NY

Cecelia Reynolds
St. Ambrose School
Boulder, CO

Miriam Rojas
St. Therese School
Alhambra, CA

Brendan Ronan
Servite High School
Anaheim, CA

C. A. Thompson-Briggs
Holy Family Academy
Manchester, NH

Perla Villasenor
St. Albert the Great
Elementary School
Rancho Dominguez, CA

How to Use This Guide

Each lesson in this Teacher's Guide is designed as a supplement. Lessons are also designed to be self-contained, so that you may just as easily present a single lesson or all of them. If you are able to teach them all, we recommend presenting them in the order they appear in the book.

Each learning topic includes:

- Lesson overview, grade level, and time
- Biblical touchstones
- Essential questions
- Connections to the *Catechism* and, where applicable, to the USCCB Curriculum Framework
- Sacred art and discussion questions
- Background reading
- Warm-up
- Activities and handouts
- Wrap-Up
- Extension options, including bulletin board ideas, where applicable
- Answer Key

Tips:

- Use the sacred art with ALL grade levels.
- Use the Biblical Touchstones for scriptural memorization.
- Let yourself be inspired by lessons even if they are not recommended for the grade you teach.
- You know best what your students already know, so keep that in mind when approaching warm-up exercises, which are meant to recall prior knowledge and/or create a mindset for the lesson.
- Grade level recommendations are merely suggestions. You know your students best.

A note on scriptural selections

The translation of the Bible used in this teacher's guide is the New American Bible, Revised Edition (NABRE). For the sake of readability on certain student handouts, we have removed biblical line breaks, line numbers, footnotes, and other references. Whenever possible, we encourage you to have students use their own copies of the Holy Bible to do readings.

Sacred Art and Catechesis
How to Use the Works of Art in This Guide

This Teacher's Guide uses sacred art as a means of teaching young people about the Catholic Faith. Beauty disposes us to the Divine, and sacred art helps lead students to love what is good, beautiful, and true. Art can be viewed and appreciated by all students, no matter their grade, reading ability, personal background, or level of sophistication. Feel free to use these works of art with students of all grade levels. Add your own questions if these are too hard. Say them out loud if students cannot read the questions themselves. Have older students compose their own questions. Have fun.

➤ Before presenting artwork, we recommend you gather relevant Scripture passages and sections of the *Catechism* to contextualize discussion. Numerous references for each artwork can be found here: **www.SophiaInstituteforTeachers.org/library/art**.

➤ We recommend projecting a full-screen image of each work of art, and/or handing out color copies for each student or small group of students.

➤ Allow students to view the art quietly for several minutes – or for as long as you can. Encourage them to appreciate it for its own sake before beginning any analysis.

➤ Begin your discussion by asking questions that are easy to answer. This may help "prime the pump" for future discussion.

➤ Be willing to share your own response to the painting. Allow your students to see the painting move you. Sharing the feelings and ideas the artwork evokes in you may encourage your students to be more willing to take risks in the ways they contribute to the discussion.

➤ Add your own favorite works of art. Don't be limited to paintings. Think about using sculpture, wood carvings, stained glass, and so forth. Your enthusiasm for works of art will be contagious.

Laminated art sets are available for purchase at **SophiaInstitute.com**.

Life in Christ Is God's Gift to Us

by Michel Therrien, STL, STD, Augustine Institute

God created us for happiness. His expressed will for us is that we attain this happiness through a holy union with Him in charity. Scripture calls this happiness beatitude or blessedness. It is a complete participation in the glory of the Trinity's own eternal communion of love and is the supreme gift God extends to each and every person He creates. The whole of salvation history bears testimony to this most fundamental truth: God wills nothing more than that we share in His own blessedness, and it is for this purpose that God created us in His image and likeness. To be created in the image of God means that we are created as personal beings capable of love and communion. God has given us the supreme dignity of freedom for the sake of this vocation to love, and when we exercise our freedom for the sake of loving God and one another we become like Him.

The gift of freedom is thus a capacity God gives to us in order to make our life a gift to others. As St. Paul tells us in his letter to the Galatians, "For you were called to freedom, brethren; only do not use your freedom as an opportunity for the flesh, but through love be servants of one another (5:13). To love in this way is to allow the image of God within us to manifest itself as God's love to the world, since, as St. John tells us, God is love (1 John 4:8).

Another word that captures this human vocation to love is holiness. To be holy is to love as God loves. The saints of the Church are declared holy precisely because of their charity. To the extent to which they gave themselves freely to God and neighbor, they became "perfect as [their] heavenly father is perfect" (Matthew 5:48). Indeed, Christians often overlook the fact that Jesus elevated and perfected the golden rule, which states, "so whatever you wish that men would do to you, do so to them" (Matthew 7:12). By making his free self-offering on the cross – the complete revelation of divine love and the measure of Christian discipleship – he is able to give us a new commandment: "that you love one another, even as I have loved you, that you also love one another. By this all men will know that you are my disciples, if you have love for one another" (John 13:34). This is the whole meaning of Christian morality – to use our freedom for the sake of charity, for self-gift.

To believe that charity is the core of Christian discipleship is to believe that our faith is principally about a relationship with God and not merely about following rules. Thus, Christian morality is relational, not relativistic. As Christ shows us, charity makes many demands of us and can only be expressed in truth. True and mature Christian charity recognizes that certain acts are evil and to be avoided because

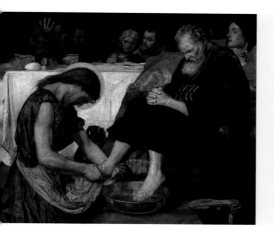

The gift of freedom is thus a capacity God gives to us in order to make our life a gift to others.

Jesus Washing Peter's Feet,
Maddox Brown

they destroy our relationship to God, our self, or our neighbor. Christian maturity is also motivated by the deepest sense of the good and not simply by 'what's in it for me.' Ultimately, it is moved to what is good by the truth and beauty of God.

Because of sin, however, to love as God loves is not easy. Every person experiences some degree of disorder within their heart, an excessive attachment to the ego, to material possessions, and to sensual pleasure (Gen 3:6). The Apostle John identifies this interior disorder with worldliness: "For all that is in the world, the lust of the flesh and the lust of the eyes and the pride of life, is not of the Father but is of the world" (1 John 2:16). This spiritual disease that tradition calls the "three-fold concupiscence" fragments the order and wholeness God established in the beginning. The challenge of becoming like God in holiness, therefore, is most evident in the experience of sin and the woundedness that follows.

Through sin we impair our capacity for love by abusing our freedom and using it for selfish purposes, even while deep within our conscience we also experience God calling us to a deeper faithfulness and obedience to the light of truth. The council fathers of Vatican II identify this call to faithful obedience with the natural law: "Deep within his conscience man discovers a law which he has not laid upon himself but which he must obey. Its voice, ever calling him to love and to do what is good and to avoid evil, tells him inwardly at the right moment: do this, shun that. For man has in his heart a law inscribed by God. His dignity lies in observing this law, and by it he will be judged" (*Gaudium et Spes*, no. 16).

Sacred Scripture reveals the profound depth of God's mercy in dealing with the problem of human sin. Therein, salvation history tells the story of how God gives humanity a variety of helps to assist us on our path to holiness. We need these helps because of the weakness with which original sin affects us. Sin not only blinds us to the truth, but it also weakens our will and disorders our natural emotional states. The first of these helps is God's law by which he guides us toward the way of life (Deuteronomy 30:19). St. Thomas Aquinas calls God's law an "exterior principle of human acts" since it serves to enlighten us along the path of holiness.

God's law is revealed to us as a teacher in the way of holiness. It was first written on stone tablets at Mount Sinai and then written anew on our hearts through the indwelling of the Holy Spirit at baptism. This gift of the Holy Spirit was foretold by the prophet Ezekiel: "I will sprinkle clean water upon you, and you shall be clean from all your uncleannesses. ... A new heart I will give you, and a new spirit I will put within you; and I will take out of your flesh the heart of stone and give you a heart of flesh. And I will put my spirit within you, and cause you to walk in my statutes and be careful to observe my ordinances" (36:25-27).

The second help God gives us is among the first fruits of our Baptism, namely, the seeds of those virtues that build us up in holiness, especially faith, hope, and charity. Aquinas calls virtue an "interior principle of human acts" because, as the good habits of faithful obedience, they form the human mind and heart in truth and goodness, helping us to overcome the interior disorders of Original Sin, especially our disintegrated emotions and earthly attachments. By infusing within us the virtues of Christian living, God empowers us to live as children of light (Ephesians 5:8) who for freedom have been set free from sin (Galatians 5:1).

These forms of assistance that God gives to us would not amount to much, however, without the redemption won for us by Jesus Christ. This is God's greatest gift to us. Through His life and death, suffering and resurrection—the Paschal Mystery—Jesus has not only exemplified perfect holiness of life, but He has also opened for us a wellspring of grace and has given "power to become children of God" (John 1:3). Jesus said of Himself "I am the Way, the Truth, and the Life" (John 14:6). In becoming one of us, and in being tempted in every way but without ever consenting to sin, the Son of God opened humanity up to the inner life of God's eternal love (Hebrews 4:15). In becoming flesh, the Word of God has raised

In the Sermon on the Mount, Jesus reveals the deepest meaning of God's law, namely, that the love of God, self, and neighbor is to proceed from a heart that is poor in spirit, sorrowful for sin, meek and hungry for justice, merciful, chaste, peaceful, and willing to suffer for the Kingdom of God.

The Sermon on the Mount, Bl. Fra Angelico

human nature up to divine life (2 Peter 1:4). This is why we call Christian morality, *Life in Christ*. In Christ, we are conceived into the eternal life of God's own Son.

During his earthly life, particularly in the Sermon on the Mount (Matthew 5-7), Jesus taught us the many ways holiness of life is to be realized. St. Augustine tells us that the Sermon holds an honored place in Christian moral instruction. Others have called Christ's Sermon the *Magna Carta* of Christian living. Jesus, the Word made flesh, reveals the deepest meaning of God's law, namely, that the love of God, self, and neighbor is to proceed from a heart that is poor in spirit, sorrowful for sin, meek and hungry for justice, merciful, chaste, peaceful, and willing to suffer for the Kingdom of God (Matthew 5:3-12). Only a heart such as this, formed in grace after Christ's own heart, is capable of fulfilling the seemingly impossible demands of Christian discipleship, for example, by loving our enemies, putting away lust, and making no allowance for anxiety so that the Kingdom of God might be first in all things. The many graces that flow from the Cross into our soul enable the members of Christ's Church to live this way and thus become salt and light for the world (Matthew 5:13-14) and a fruitful witness to the Kingdom of God.

When Christian discipleship is placed within the proper context of charity and relationship, we are able to move beyond a purely legalistic faith. Throughout the centuries, Christians have been tempted to reduce the Christian life to a moral code of conduct by which we see discipleship as a matter of compliance to rules and motivated by a sense of guilt and obligation. In this paradigm we see God as a Master that requires a moral regiment of external practices that lack any reference to interior transformation or interpersonal communion with God. This way of living can easily become formalistic, rigid and devoid of spiritual fruit.

Therefore, the key to living in Christ and receiving this life as a gift is prayer. Through prayer the disciple communes with God and entrusts his life to God's loving providence. Prayer is how we meet the gaze of our loving Savior who longs to renew us from within and release us from the bondage of sin. When we encounter Him in prayer, the Divine Physician heals our interior wounds, insecurities, and weaknesses.

The liturgy offers us the supreme opportunity for this communion with God. All the sacraments that flow from the Church's liturgical life are an invitation from Christ to encounter his love and receive the spiritual nourishment that renews us and restores us to the happiness for which God made us and the fullness of life. In his Bread of Life discourse from John 6, Jesus tells us, "He who eats my flesh and drinks my blood has eternal life, and I will raise him up at the last day. For my flesh is food indeed, and my blood is drink indeed. He who eats my flesh and drinks my blood abides in me, and I in him" (John 6:54-56).

Thus, the Sacrament of the Eucharist holds a privileged place in Christian discipleship. Yet, so too, does the Sacrament of Reconciliation. When the Lord reconciles us to himself, we encounter his mercy, as did the woman caught in adultery: "Neither do I condemn you; go, and do not sin again" (John 8:11). By these two fonts of grace, the divine life of Christ is built up in us and draws us more deeply into the Trinity's own inner life of blessedness. It is into this most holy place that Jesus calls us when he asks us to follow Him. The challenge of the moral life is simply to respond generously to His call.

Dr. Michel Therrien is the Secretary of Evangelization and Catholic Education for the Diocese of Pittsburgh. He also serves as a visiting professor of Fundamental Moral Theology of the Augustine Institute. He taught at St. Vincent Seminary in Latrobe, Pennsylvania, for 7 years, serving as Academic Dean from 2008-2012. His prior work experience includes teaching high school religion, serving as a DRE, a youth minister, and RCIA leader for various parishes. He has also led adult faith formation in various parishes since 2003. He holds a B.A. in theology from Gonzaga University in Spokane, Washington, an M.A. in theology and Christian ministry from Franciscan University of Steubenville, a Licentiate in sacred theology from the International Theological Institute in Gaming, Austria, and a Doctorate in fundamental moral theology from the University of Fribourg in Switzerland.

Our Ultimate End Is Heaven

Overview

This lesson introduces the ideas of who we are and what we are. The fact that we are made in the image and likeness of God calls for us to do certain things. We are called to self-discovery, and we look to our Creator to discover who we are. Students will learn that we have free will, and that there are laws that govern heaven, the universe, the earth and the human person. In learning these things, we can discover our true ends and purposes in beatitude.

Grade Levels

 MS ■ HS

Time

Three fifty-minute classes

Note: This lesson is designed as a unit, and includes three parts: Day I: The Imago Dei [HS]; Day II: What Is Law? [HS]; and Day III: What Is Freedom? [MS, HS]

Connection to the Catechism

- › CCC 355
- › CCC 1950-1960
- › CCC 1730-1733
- › CCC 1747
- › CCC 1748

Essential Questions

- › If we are created in God's image, then how should we conduct ourselves?
- › What is law?
- › How does the world's definition of "freedom" differ from the Church's understanding? Which is right?
- › What did Jesus mean when He said "the truth will set you free"?

BIBLICAL TOUCHSTONES

God created mankind in his image, in the image of God he created them; male and female he created them.

GENESIS 1:27

If you remain in my word, you will truly be my disciples and you will know the truth and the truth will set you free.

JOHN 8:31-32

The Creation of Adam

BY MICHELANGELO BUONARROTI (C. 1511)

Sacred Art and the Beatitudes
Our Ultimate End Is Heaven

The Creation of Adam, by *Michelangelo Buonarroti* (c. 1511)

Directions: Take some time to quietly view and reflect on the art. Let yourself be inspired in any way that happens naturally. Then think about the questions below, and discuss them with your classmates.

Conversation Questions

1. Whom do you see in this fresco, and what appears to be happening?

2. What do you notice about the colors the artist chose? How does the light look? Where is it coming from?

3. What are some feelings that this painting inspires in you?

4. How does Adam's posture differ from the Father's?

5. Why do you think Michelangelo painted the Father's hand and Adam's hand almost, but not quite, touching?

6. Who do you think are the figures with the Father? Why do you think so?

7. Read Genesis 1:26-27. How does this painting enhance your understanding of these verses?

8. Some physicians have suggested that the shape behind God the Father resembles the outline of a human brain. If this is true, why might Michelangelo have painted it that way?

9. How does this painting depict the ultimate end for which we are created?

Day One Lesson Plan
The Imago Dei

Materials

> Holy Bible

> *Catechism of the Catholic Church*

> A musical instrument and a recorded piece of music for that instrument

> Background Essay: Our Ultimate End Is Heaven

> Essential Vocabulary

> Handout A: The Is/Ought Connection

> Handout B: Plato on the Three Parts of the Soul

> Handout C: St. Gregory the Great, On the Making of Man, Part V

Background/Homework — *15 minutes*

Read aloud the **Background Essay** as students follow along. Students should reflect on the conversation questions.

Warm-Up — *10 minutes*

A. The fact/value distinction is an is/ought connection. Discuss with students how a thing can be known by science or reason. By fact of that understanding, we are called to act in a way concerning that thing. The example in the Background Essay is that when we see a man **is** hungry, we **ought** to feed him.

B. Distribute **Handout A: The Is/Ought Connection.** On the worksheet, students should derive an "ought to do" statement from each stated fact.

C. Discuss variations in answers. If there are wildly varying ideas, try to reason out why we wouldn't have similar response.

Activity — *30 Minutes*

A. Discuss the following question: What is the nature of being human?

B. Pass out **Handout B: Plato on the Three Parts of the Soul**. Examine the Greek Philosopher Plato's tripartite soul comprising the belly, head, and heart. Observe how Plato's theory of the tripartite is a little trinity. Discuss the similarities between the two conceptions and graphics. Lead them into the idea that man is made in the image and likeness of God.

C. Discuss the following question: What does it mean to be made in the image and likeness of God?

D. Have students open their Bibles and turn to the first chapter of Genesis and read 1:27. Read and discuss the nature of man being made in the image and likeness of God. Conclude that God created humans and therefore humans are creatures of God. Discuss also that it is in our intellect and will, not in our physical features, that we are made in the image of God.

E. St. Gregory explains a little bit about what it means to be in the image and likeness of God. The two faculties of the Soul – the intellect and the will – are the proper way to understand this sacred image. Read and discuss **Handout C: St. Gregory the Great, On the Making of Man, Part V** in class.

F. Make a point of clarification: by way of analogy to the artist and color, St. Gregory demonstrates that God's artistry and color are not of the physical realm, but that of the intellect and will by way of the Logos and Love, of word and mind, of act and free will.

Wrap up

10 minutes

Recall the is/ought connection. What something **is** tells us what we **ought** to do. So, the facts are that God created us. We are made in His image and likeness in terms of our intellect and will. Therefore we must discover the rules God has made for us because he made us and he who makes a thing makes the laws that govern that thing.

Wrap up by developing a thesis to explain what the fact of our created status means we ought to do. Make the following chart on the board.

Fact	What we ought to do in response to this fact
We are made in the Image and likeness of God	This means we ought to…..

Day Two Lesson Plan
What Is Law?

Materials

> Holy Bible

> *Catechism of the Catholic Church*

> Handout D: The Four Laws

Warm-Up
10 minutes

A. What is a law? Write on the board: St. Thomas Aquinas says a "law is a rule and measure of acts, whereby man is induced to act or is restrained from acting."

B. Discuss the concept of laws as rules that impel us to act or to restrain from acting.

C. Are there different kinds of laws? Answer: Yes, eternal law, divine law, natural law and human law.

Activity
30 Minutes

A. Write the following statement on the board and explain that this is what Aquinas says of human law:

> *"A law is an ordinance of reason promulgated by the proper authority for the common good."*

Dissect every word of this statement by Thomas Aquinas and quickly define each key word so that by mental eyes and hooks the students can see how these words are connected to point to a deeper understanding of the notion of a law. Use the **Essential Vocabulary** resource if needed.

B. The Four Laws

   1. Pass out **Handout D: The Four Laws**. If possible, project it onto the board using an overhead projector or a touchscreen.

   2. Use the chart to define and make distinctions between the four kinds of laws as St. Thomas Aquinas explicates them.

3. Draw students into a discussion about the relationship of the laws and notice that the human law is the only law that can be at variance with the perfect harmony of eternal, divine and natural.

4. Conclude that St. Thomas Aquinas points out that when human law is not in accord with the law written on our hearts, we have a responsibility not to follow it, as in the case of legalized abortion. That abortion is legal does not mean it is good.

Wrap up

10 minutes

Discuss other such laws that may not be in accord with natural law. Try to determine whether or not we are free to obey the different types of laws.

Day Three Lesson Plan
What Is Freedom?

Materials

> Holy Bible

> *Catechism of the Catholic Church*

> Handout E: Jesus Christ's Lesson on Freedom

> St. Thomas Aquinas, *Summa Theologica*, Question 90—On The Essence of Law (optional)

Background/Homework   *15 minutes*

Have students write a brief reflection paper on the questions: What is Freedom? What does it mean to be free? Christ said "the truth will set you free." What did He mean by that?

Warm-Up   *5 minutes*

A. Freedom is a very misunderstood concept today. Point out that there are at least two different understandings of freedom: that of the world and that of the Church.

B. Demonstrate an overview of the worldly view as expressed by the American Heritage Dictionary.

The World's View of Freedom
American Heritage Dictionary says:

> The condition of not being in prison or captivity

> The condition of being free of restraints, especially the ability to act without control or interference by another or by circumstance

> The condition of not being constrained or restricted in a specific aspect of life by a government or other power

> The condition of not being affected or restricted by a given circumstance or condition

> The condition of not being bound by established conventions or rules

> The capacity to act by choice rather than by determination, as from fate or a deity

> The right to unrestricted use; full access

> *Archaic*: Boldness in behavior; lack of modesty or reserve

Conclude that the above is not really freedom, but licentiousness. To be untethered from every rule and constraint is a "freedom" from everything, but this kind of "freedom" is a form of slavery that binds one to sin.

Activity I
10 Minutes

A. With an instrument in the room (a piano, guitar, cello, or any available instrument), seek out a student who is not a musical virtuoso. Ask the unmusical student to "play something beautiful." (The idea is that the student, because he/she is not musical, is unable to play something beautiful.)

B. Next play a recording of a virtuoso artist playing a single instrument, such as Segovia playing classical guitar, or Yo-Yo Ma playing the cello. Enjoy the aesthetic beauty of the virtuosos.

C. As all students should easily notice which was better, ask them *"Who is freer in the area of musical expression? Our classmate? Or the virtuoso?"*

D. Draw their attention to the fact that the virtuoso by arduous adherence to the laws and nature of music and committed practice aimed at perfection is freer to express beauty by the instrument. There is a relationship between our instrumentalities in our own ends by participating in the eternal law if we are to end in perfect beatitude.

Activity II
20 minutes

A. Pass out **Handout E: Jesus Christ's Lesson on Freedom.**

B. Before you begin the exercise, it is important to remind the students to remember that there are rules for how we are to properly read Scripture. In the *Catechism* we can learn that the Holy Spirit is the one who interprets the Holy Scriptures and as such we are bound by three rules found in the *Catechism* paragraphs 109-114.

   1. We must not take things out of context and "be especially attentive to the content and unity of the whole Scripture."

   2. We must "read the Scripture within "the living Tradition of the whole Church."

   3. We must "be attentive to the analogy of faith."

C. Work through **Handout E** trying to interpret what Christ means by using the word "free." By discussion this should naturally lead to a discernment of the Church's understanding of freedom. What Christ means by "freedom" is a freedom from sin, defect, and error, and freedom to be holy by virtuous acts.

D. Open the *Catechism* to paragraph 1730. Use these summary points to discuss Christ's freedom:

1743 "God willed that man should be left in the hand of his own counsel (cf. *Sir* 15:14), so that he might of his own accord seek his creator and freely attain his full and blessed perfection by cleaving to him" (GS 17 § 1).

1744 Freedom is the power to act or not to act, and so to perform deliberate acts of one's own. Freedom attains perfection in its acts when directed toward God, the sovereign Good.

1745 Freedom characterizes properly human acts. It makes the human being responsible for acts of which he is the voluntary agent. His deliberate acts properly belong to him.

1746 The imputability or responsibility for an action can be diminished or nullified by ignorance, duress, fear, and other psychological or social factors.

1747 The right to the exercise of freedom, especially in religious and moral matters, is an inalienable requirement of the dignity of man. But the exercise of freedom does not entail the putative right to say or do anything.

1748 "For freedom Christ has set us free" (Galatians 5:1).

Activity III   *10 minutes*

Make a chart on the board comparing the world's freedom to Christ's freedom by considering "freedom from" and "freedom to." Note that these two freedoms end in being diametrically opposed to one another, similar to the two musicians. Add to this chart in the discussion as is appropriate.

The Freedom of the World		The Freedom of Christ	
Freedom To	**Freedom From**	**Freedom To**	**Freedom From**
➤ Do whatever one wants ➤ Sin ➤ Cultivate vice	➤ Rules ➤ Virtue ➤ Cultivating good habits	➤ Follow rules – eternal/divine law ➤ Pursue virtue ➤ Cultivate good habits	➤ Slavery to appetites ➤ Sin ➤ Unhealthy distractions

Wrap-up

Have students open their *Catechisms* to paragraph 27 to learn about our purpose in life. Read along with them:

> "*The desire for God is written in the human heart, because man is created by God and for God; and God never ceases to draw man to himself. Only in God will he find the truth and happiness he never stops searching for.*"

God made us and we are intended to end with God. Our final purpose is to end in beatitude, eternal happiness with God.

St. Thomas Aquinas tells us that the fulfillment of beatitude, the highest form of human happiness we call blessedness, is "to possess God in full in the beatific vision, to have our powers fully realized, fully perfected, and to find them at rest, in perfect happiness for all eternity face to face with God."

This is our end, it is our final purpose, and it is greatly to be desired. Before we can begin our life's work of attaining our final beatitude, we must prepare our hearts, minds, and souls with the preceding three lessons:

1. We are created by God, in His image and Likeness, we are Imago Dei and this fact calls us to act in accordance to His governance.

2. God is the author of life and of this universe and as such it is His authority by which all laws are promulgated. If we are to end in heaven we must recognize the distinction between the human law, prone to error, and the perfect eternal law that is forever true and unchanging.

3. We must recognize our gift of free will and the true nature of freedom intended for us by Christ and we must notice the diametrically opposite notion of freedom adopted by the world. We must embrace the freedom of Christ and reject the freedom of the world.

In taking these three lessons to heart, we prepare ourselves for our final beatific end in Heaven.

Homework

Have students write a reflection paper meditating on how the elements of Imago Dei, the four laws, freedom, and our end in beatitude are all tied together. Have advanced students read St. Thomas Aquinas, *Summa Theologica*, Question 90 – On The Essence of Law.

Our Ultimate End Is Heaven

It is a universal law of truth that certain facts call for certain obligatory actions. Christ tells us that if a man is hungry we ought to feed him. He tells us that if a man is thirsty, we ought to give him drink. He tells us that if a man is naked, we ought to clothe him (Matthew 25:31-46). These corporal works of mercy illustrate the is/ought connection that has become less apparent in modern times. How we should act flows from the way things are. The fact that we are made in the image and likeness of God reveals our intrinsic dignity. It also calls us to certain moral courses of action that will lead us to our proper end, which is eternal life with the Blessed Trinity in Heaven.

Imago Dei

In Genesis 1:27 it is clearly stated that "God created man in his own image, in the image of God he created him." We are created in the image and likeness of God, and we ought to discover what this means. To further elucidate these revealed facts we read in paragraph 354 of the Catechism that "of all visible creatures only man is able to know and love his creator. He is the only creature on earth that God has willed for its own sake, and he alone is called to share, by knowledge and love, in God's own life. It was for this end that he was created." We are moral agents with free will. Because we have intellect and will, the very image of God, we are obligated to discover the laws that

Creation, Giusto de' Menabuoi

govern the Cosmos and to follow them if we intend to end as our Creator desires it for us.

So by virtue of our being made in God's own image and likeness, we have been graced with intellect and will. By our intellect we are obligated to discern whether or not our actions, thoughts, and intentions correspond to God's actions, thoughts and intentions. By our further gift of free will, we are able to choose or reject the laws we discover and even the purpose God intends for us.

St. Thomas Aquinas and the Four Kinds of Law

To accept that we are created in the Image of God and imbued with free will leads us to ask "how than shall we live?" To live authentically as God intends for us we must discover the laws that govern human existence. St. Thomas Aquinas explains in question 90 of the *Summa Theologica* that a "law is a rule and measure of acts, whereby man is induced to act or is restrained from acting." He explains that the etymological root of law, lex, comes from the verb "ligare" which means "to bind." So in essence, laws are those rules to which we bind ourselves to determine the course of human action. Law is something profoundly good. It is the pathway that leads us toward what is good. The law leads to human flourishing in this life and eternal life in the next.

St. Thomas goes on to explain that there are four kinds of law: eternal, divine, natural and human.

The eternal law is God's conception of reality that is outside time and space. It is the source of all laws that corresponds to ultimate reality and truth.

Natural law is man's participation in the eternal law by the right use of reason. Natural law is the law written into human nature by virtue of being created. It can be known by human reason, and so it is a law common to all human beings regardless of when they lived, their religion or culture. We find that God's Law is written on our hearts by natural law.

Divine law is the law that comes to us from God's revelation in history, begun with the law given to Moses on Mount Sinai, continuing through the prophets (the "Old Law") and brought to fulfillment by Christ Himself (the "New Law" or the "Law of the Gospel"). Divine law is further elucidated by the Saints, particularly the Church Doctors and our Magisterium (CCC 1961-1974).

Human law is the set of laws men make by their own powers, such as the laws of various federal, state and local governments. The Church also has her own law, called "ecclesiastical law" or "canon law." These laws are made to help promote the common good, helping everyone to live in harmony with God and each other and leading to human flourishing and happiness. These laws must never contradict the eternal, natural and divine law.

An understanding of all four types of laws is essential for living out God's intended purpose for us and for living together in harmony (also called "the common good").

The Freedom of Christ

Once we discover that we were created in the image and likeness of God and that by the right use of reason we can participate in eternal law, we can come to appreciate the nature of the freedom with which God has imbued every human soul. God does not force us to obey him and we are free to choose obedience or rejection. The freedom of Christ is the freedom to seek goodness, truth and beauty by way of the virtues perfectly embodied by Christ.

The world mistakenly thinks freedom is to do whatever one wants unhindered by limits and rules. But in truth, this type of "freedom" is really the opposite of freedom. It makes one a slave to sin. Christ's freedom makes one truly free, for as he said in John 6: "the truth will set you free." The freedom of Christ is to choose virtue and to avoid the slavery of sin. In Galatians 5:13-15, St. Paul explains, "For you were called for freedom, brothers. But do not use this freedom as an opportunity for the flesh; rather, serve one another through love. For the whole law is fulfilled in one statement, namely, 'You shall love your neighbor as yourself.'" In other words, following God's law gives us the freedom to love authentically both God and our neighbor.

If understand that we are created in the image of God, the four laws, and the true nature of freedom, we will then be ready to embrace our final end of Beatitude. Aquinas explains that beatitude lies in the contemplation of truth. There is no separation between the right use of reason and the will that loves and desires. If we submit our wills to the will of the creator and choose love of God over love of ourselves, we will end as God intended for us. St. Thomas Aquinas tells us that "to possess God in full in the beatific vision is to have our powers fully realized, fully perfected, and to find them at rest, in perfect happiness for all eternity." Let us know ourselves as Imago Dei and use our freedom to follow the law written on our hearts so that we may end in Heaven in eternal beatitude.

Conversation Questions

1. Describe the implications of the is/ought connection. How does it apply to the Corporal and Spiritual Works of Mercy?
2. What does it mean to be made in the Image of God?
3. What are the four laws?
4. Explain what Christ means when He says "the truth will set you free."
5. What is the nature of freedom according to the world? According to the Church? How do these understandings differ? Which is right?

Essential Vocabulary

›   **Imago Dei:** This phrase is Latin for "image of God." We are rational and capable of love because we are made in the image and likeness of God.

›   **Eternal law:** The source of all law, the eternal and unchanging Truth outside of time and space.

›   **Divine law:** The revelation of the eternal law by way of the Old and New Testament, especially the Logos, Christ himself. Its clearest exposition is found in the Sacred Scriptures and the Magisterium of Holy Mother Church.

›   **Natural law:** Man's participation in the eternal law by reading what is written upon our hearts. It is unchanging, and "permanent throughout history" (CCC 1978).

›   **Human law:** Man's reasonable interpretation of the natural law to reduce its general principles into specific and concrete ordinances to deal with day-to-day living and governance.

›   **Ordinance:** An authoritative order or decree.

›   **Reason:** The power of our minds to think and form judgments according to logic. Promulgate: To put a law, decree, or an order into effect by official proclamation.

›   **Proper:** Truly what something is understood or regarded to be – genuine.

›   **Authority:** "The quality or virtue by which persons or institutions make laws and give orders and expect men to obey and follow them" (CCC 1897).

›   **Common good:** The sum total of social conditions that best allows all persons to reach their fulfillment. The common good includes such things as protecting life and promoting peace by way of justice.

The Is/Ought Connection

Directions: For every "is" statement, provide an "ought to" action.

	The fact of a thing and what it is:	What we ought to do in response to this fact:
1	You see a starving man on the side of the road as you walk by.	
2	You run across a man dying of thirst in the desert.	
3	Your little sister falls off her bike and skins her knee.	
4	Someone makes a racist comment to your friend.	
5	An elderly lady trips and falls in front of you on the sidewalk.	
6	Someone wants to learn something that you know.	
7	On a hot summer day you see a baby locked in a car.	
8	Someone asks you for advice on whether or not they should steal something.	
9	Someone is sick and in need of care.	
10	Someone is in financial dire straits.	
11	Someone is lonely.	
12	You see someone get bullied.	

Plato on the Three Parts of the Soul

Plato's theory of the tripartite (three-part) soul simply denoted by **belly**, **head**, and **heart** is a brilliant place to start to begin to understand what is common to all human persons considering our universal human nature.

Plato's three elements of the soul are:

1. Plato associates the **appetites** with the **belly**. Our belly is a symbol of hunger, desire, and the element by which we express the wants and desires satisfied by material things. When we "hunger for" things, we usually associate that with the belly.

2. Plato associates the **will** with the **heart**. With our hearts, we choose to love, act, and find courage to overcome great trials.

3. Plato associates the **intellect** with the **head**. This faculty of the soul is that by which we come to know the good and bad of things. Through understanding, judgment and reason, the mind informs the will as to how it ought to act. It is also by the mind that the will moderates the appetites.

Plato's tripartite conception of the human person bears a striking resemblance to the Catholic understanding of the Trinity.

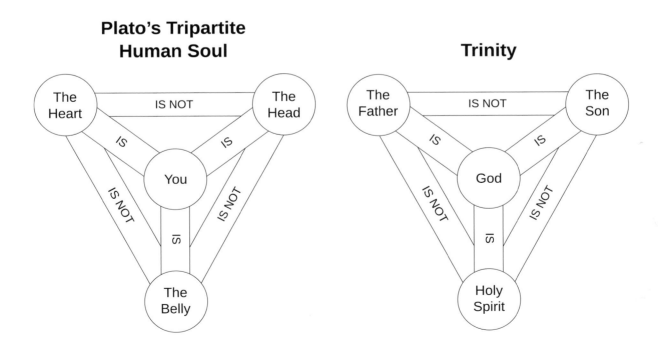

Plato's Tripartite Human Soul

Trinity

St. Gregory the Great, On the Making of Man, Part V

■

That man is a likeness of the Divine sovereignty.

1. It is true, indeed, that the Divine beauty is not adorned with any shape or endowment of form, by any beauty of color, but is contemplated as excellence in unspeakable bliss. As the painters transfer human forms to their pictures by the means of certain colors, laying on their copy the proper and corresponding tints, so that the beauty of the original may be accurately transferred to the likeness, so I would have you understand that our Maker also, painting the portrait to resemble His own beauty, by the addition of virtues, as it were with colours, shows in us His own sovereignty: and manifold and varied are the tints, so to say, by which His true form is portrayed: not red, or white, or the blending of these, whatever it may be called, nor a touch of black that paints the eyebrow and the eye, and shades, by some combination, the depressions in the figure, and all such arts which the hands of painters contrive, but instead of these, purity, freedom from passion, blessedness, alienation from all evil, and all those attributes of the like kind which help to form in men the likeness of God: with such hues as these did the Maker of His own image mark our nature.

2. And if you were to examine the other points also by which the Divine beauty is expressed, you will find that to them too the likeness in the image which we present is perfectly preserved. The Godhead is mind and word: for in the beginning was the Word and the followers of Paul have the mind of Christ which speaks in them: humanity too is not far removed from these: you see in yourself word and understanding, an imitation of the very Mind and Word. Again, God is love, and the fount of love: for this the great John declares, that love is of God, and God is love (1 John 4:7-8): the Fashioner of our nature has made this to be our feature too: for hereby, He says, shall all men know that you are my disciples, if you love one another: – thus, if this be absent, the whole stamp of the likeness is transformed. The Deity beholds and hears all things, and searches all things out: you too have the power of apprehension of things by means of sight and hearing, and the understanding that inquires into things and searches them out.

The Four Laws

> **Definition of Law:** A law is a rule or measure, rooted in reason and laid down by the ruler of a community, that encourages people to act or restrains their actions.

1

Eternal Law

The eternal law is the divine governance of all things. Being outside of time and space, the eternal law is the divine source of all laws.

2

Divine Law

Divine law is the eternal law that has been revealed to us by Bible, the prophets, the saints, and particularly by Christ, who is the revealed Word of God.

3

Natural Law

Natural law is man's participation in the eternal law. It can be discovered through reason across history and culture.

4

Human Law

Human law is a set of rules relating to human conduct. It is created using reason, drawing on our understanding of the general principles of eternal and natural law.

Conclusion: Eternal law is unchanging Truth; divine law is an explanation of the eternal law through revelation; natural law is man's participation in the eternal law written on our hearts; and human law is particular rules drawn out as "an ordinance of reason for the common good," made and enforced by a ruler or government. Aquinas warns that we are not bound to obey laws made by humans which conflict with natural law.

Jesus Christ's Lesson on Freedom

The Church's sense of freedom is diametrically opposed to the world's sense of freedom. If we turn to Christ, we can learn of the Church's sense.

Many times, people in the world take Christ's words out of their context and try to make them mean what Christ did not intend.

In John 8:32 Christ's words "the truth will set you free" are often repeated by those in and out of the Church. In the box below, describe what you think Jesus meant when He said:

> **"The truth will set you free" (John 8:32)**
>
> What does Jesus mean by "free"?

If you are not sure, then we ought to ask "What came before this?" And we can add the line before it.

> **"and you will know the truth, and the truth will set you free" (John 8:32)**
>
> Does this change what you think Jesus means by "free"?

Perhaps we should go back further.

> **"you will truly be my disciples and you will know the truth, and the truth will set you free" (John 8:31-32)**
>
> Does this change what you think Jesus means by "free"?

Perhaps we should go back even further.

"If you remain in my word, you will truly be my disciples and you will know the truth, and the truth will set you free" (John 8:31-32).

Now write down what Christ meant by "free."

Conclusion

What Christ means by "freedom" is a freedom from sin, defect, and error, and freedom to be holy by virtuous acts. The *Catechism* illustrates the nature of freedom in paragraphs 1730-1734.

Answer Key

Sacred Art and the Beatitudes

1. Students may say that God the Father and Adam are reaching out toward each other. God the Father appears to have just created Adam.

2. Accept reasoned answers.

3. Accept reasoned answers.

4. God the Father is looking directly at Adam. The Father appears strong, forceful, and determined, especially compared to Adam who seems more relaxed. Adam is reclining, and his head is tilted slightly to the side.

5-9. Accept reasoned answers.

10. This painting shows Adam, a creature of God, with God the Father. Our eternal end is in heaven.

Background Essay

1. The way reasoning is can tell us what we ought to do. In the Corporal and Spiritual Works of Mercy, Jesus gives us concrete examples of what we ought to do in response to certain facts, e.g. a man is hungry; we ought to feed him.

2. We are created in love, with intellect and free will.

3. Eternal law, divine law, natural law, human law

4. Jesus means the truth will free us from sin. Jesus is the Way, the Truth, and the Life, and we can freely choose to cooperate with His grace. He frees us to be holy.

5. The world tends to think freedom means having no rules or restraints, and the ability to do whatever one wants. The Church understands that true freedom means freedom from sin, and the freedom to cultivate virtue. The example in the lesson plan provides additional guidance.

Rules and Freedom

Overview

In Genesis, we encounter God creating mankind in His image and likeness. Not much later, man damages this likeness by committing Original Sin. Original Sin made our human condition frail and we became inclined toward sin. Throughout Scripture, God provides rules and encourages persistent adherence to them as a remedy against sin. Following these rules does not bind us down; rather, following rules bring us closer to embracing the likeness of God in ourselves and in others so that at the Last Judgment, Christ can complete the restoration of our soul to Paradise.

Connection to the Catechism

› CCC 1706

Essential Questions

› What does it mean to be created in the image of God?

› Why does God provide rules for us?

› Rules limit "freedom," don't they? How can following God's rules set me free?

Grade Level

 ES

Time

One fifty-minute class

BIBLICAL TOUCHSTONES

You shall love the Lord, your God, with all your heart, with all your soul, and with all your mind. This is the greatest and the first commandment. The second is like it: You shall love your neighbor as yourself.

MATTHEW 22:37-29

For freedom Christ set us free; so stand firm and do not submit again to the yoke of slavery.

GALATIANS 5:1

Creation of Adam

BY HARTMANN SCHEDE (1493)

Sacred Art and the Beatitudes
Rules and Freedom

Creation of Adam, *by Hartmann Schede (1493)*

Directions: Take some time to quietly view and reflect on the art. Let yourself be inspired in any way that happens naturally. Then think about the questions below, and discuss them with your classmates.

Conversation Questions

1. Whom and what do you see in this illustration?

2. What appears to be happening?

3. Where does your eye go when you look at the illustration? What is the most interesting thing?

4. What do you notice about the colors the artist chose? How does the light look? Where is it coming from?

5. What are some feelings that this illustration inspires in you?

6. Why do you think the artist painted Adam the way he did?

7. Read Genesis 2:7. How does this illustration help you understand this verse?

Lesson Plan

Materials

- 4-5, 2 x 11 strips of paper for each student
- Stapler
- Handout A: What Could You Do?
- Handout B: Key Sheet

Warm-Up   *15 minutes*

A. Share the following quotation with students: "Watch your thoughts, they become your words; watch your words, they become actions; watch your actions, they become habits; watch your habits, they become character; watch your character, for it becomes your destiny."

B. Ask the children to explain what a habit is — an action or thought that is repeated often and becomes a pattern of behavior. The more the habit is reinforced, the easier it becomes to do. Ask students to identify several examples of actions that are good habits.

C. Distribute 4-5 strips of 2 x 11 paper to each student and instruct them to write down an action that is NOT a positive habit. [Younger learners can draw a simple picture, or say a word aloud while you write it down for them.)

D. Bend each strip of paper to create a circle, staple, and interlock them to create a chain. As you do so, invite students to share some of what they chose to write down on their papers.

Activity   *20 minutes*

A. Now that you have a visual representation of the "yoke of slavery" (Galatians 5:1) that is sin, ask students what this chain represents. Discuss that the chain of our sins weighs us down and limits our actions. Note that just as a reinforced habit is easier to do, it is also difficult to break free from. Discuss how the actions on the strips of paper might seem to bring instant gratification, but the long-term consequences of the action ultimately do not provide freedom.

B. Read aloud the account of the expulsion from Eden – Genesis 2:15-17, 3:1-24.

C. Discuss what changed about Adam and Eve after they disobeyed God's one law. Original Sin damaged mankind and made the human condition frail and susceptible to sin.

D. Note that God gave humans rules to protect their dignity from the snare of sin and to empower them to love God and others.

   1. Ask students if they can think of any examples.

   2. Instruct students that God's rules can be found throughout Scripture. For example:

      ➤ The Ten Commandments

      ➤ The Corporal Works of Mercy

      ➤ The Beatitudes

      ➤ The golden rule

E. Present the verse Matthew 22:37-39 to students and discuss how this verse is a key to unlocking the chain created in the warm-up activity. Perhaps write the verse on a key constructed out of poster board as a visual. Note that God's rule doesn't weigh us down; it does the opposite: it frees us!

Wrap-Up Activity/Assessment   *15 minutes*

A. Distribute **Handout A: What Could You Do?** (1 of 3) to students so that they can independently or in groups read the scenario and respond to the critical thinking questions.

B. Invite students to share their responses with the class. Reinforce points about how Scripture helped to free the individual from the temptation to sin and make a choice of love.

C. Discuss with students how in each case, obeying God's rules and making the right choice leads not to *less* freedom, but to *more*. (And this is true in the case of day-to-day life as well as spiritually.) Philip will be free to go further in math if he studies and learns rather than cheats. Justin will be freer because he won't be grounded for disobeying; Meredith will be free from coercion from her "friends.")

D. Close by praying the second Bible verse for memorization with the students (Galatians 5:1).

Extension Options

A. Complete the musical instrument activity from the lesson "What Is Freedom" on page 8. How does a virtuoso become a virtuoso? By acting as though there are no rules? No — by following the rules of how to play an instrument: learning to read music, practicing regularly, etc. Discuss how rules and discipline create more freedom and not less.

B. Send home **Handout B: Keys** with this note:

Dear parents,

Your child has learned about how the Word of God provides true freedom by discouraging sinful actions and habits. With your child, look up three passages from Scripture pertaining to rules. The Books of Exodus, the Gospels, as well as the exhortations provided in the New Testament letters to the early Christian churches are wonderful places to start. Write each verse on one of the keys on the sheet provided and send to school for our bulletin board. Talk about the verses with your child — how do we follow the rule and how does it protect us from temptation?

Bulletin Board Extension

Create a bulletin board that illustrates how the laws, rules, and exhortations provided in Scripture free us to love and are keys that unlock the bonds of sin. The keys contain the verses that students explored and discussed with their parents in **Extension B**.

What Could You Do?

1 Philip has not been getting good grades on his math tests. His parents threatened to not let him play on his tennis team if he doesn't start doing better. Philip's friend Zach is an excellent math student — he usually gets all of the problems correct, and he happens to sit next to Philip in class. Philip did not study for this week's test and is considering looking at Zach's paper during the test. What should he do? After all, it is only a couple of math problems.

Questions

1. What is the temptation that Philip faces?

2. What are the choices — good and bad — that Philip could make?

3. Look up Exodus 20:15. How could this Scripture passage help Philip to make the right choice?

2 Justin and his friends are at a new level in the video game Justin received for his birthday. If Justin earns just a few more points, he'll win. Justin hears his dad say that it is time to turn off the video game to get ready for dinner. Justin's friend turns up the volume on the TV — the game is just too much fun. Justin could pretend that he didn't hear his Dad and finish the game. What should he do? After all, it would only be another 5 minutes.

Questions

1. What is the temptation that Justin faces?

2. What are the choices — good and bad — that Justin could make?

3. Look up Exodus 20:12. How could this Scripture passage help Justin to make the right choice?

3 Some of Meredith's friends have started using bad language. At recess, Meredith hears phrases that she knows her parents, teachers, and priest would find inappropriate. One friend even uses the name of God as if it were a bad word. Meredith's friends have started to make fun of her because she won't use the words. They tell her if she wants to be cool and stay their friend, she will have to use at least one bad word next recess. What should she do? After all, it is only one word.

Questions

1. What is the temptation that Meredith faces?

2. What are the choices — good and bad — that Meredith could make?

3. Look up Leviticus 19:12. How could this Scripture passage help Meredith to make the right choice?

HANDOUT B
Keys

Directions: Look up three passages from Scripture pertaining to rules. The Books of Exodus, the Gospels, as well as the exhortations provided in the letters to the early Christian Churches are wonderful places to start. Write each verse on one of the keys.

Answer Key

Sacred Art and the Beatitudes: Rules and Freedom

1. God the Father, a person seeming to rise out of dust, animals, a landscape, trees.
2. God is creating Adam.
3-7. Accept reasoned answers.

Handout A: What Could You Do?

Version 1

1. Philip is tempted to cheat on his test. If he does so, he would be stealing someone else's work.
2. Philip could cheat and earn a better grade that would let him continue to play tennis or Philip could take the bad grade and suffer the consequences. He could then perhaps resolve to study harder.
3. Exodus 20:15 commands us not to steal. Philip, therefore, should not cheat on the test.

Version 2

1. Justin is tempted to ignore the reasonable directions of his parent.
2. Justin could continue to play his video game and win or listen to his Dad and lose the game to his friend. Justin could also tell his friend that it is important that he listen to his dad.
3. Exodus 20:12 commands us to honor our parents. Justin, therefore, should stop playing the video game – he could always pause the game or have a rematch at a later time.

Version 3

1. Meredith is tempted to use curse words and possibly use the Lord's name in vain.
2. Meredith could use a bad word and earn the approval of her peers or she could choose not to use those words and risk losing her friends. Meredith could also speak up to her friends or teacher about the bad language.
3. Leviticus 19:12 – given instead of Exodus 20:7 for the sake of challenging students to look throughout the Bible – commands us never to take the Lord's name in vain. Meredith, therefore, should not use this foul language and should discourage her friends from using it as well.

Conscience: God's Voice in Our Hearts

Overview

Many people think that a conscience is like Jiminy Cricket. Some envision a "good angel" and a "bad angel" sitting on opposite shoulders, whispering differing advice. But conscience is much more than an "inner voice" or feeling. It is God's voice in our very hearts, if we are only able to listen to Him. A well-formed conscience helps us live as the Lord lives, and lead a holy life.

Grade Levels

 ES MS HS

Time

One fifty-minute class

Connection to the Catechism

> CCC 1776-1778

Essential Questions

> What is conscience, and what is its role in our moral life?

> How do we form our conscience according to what is good?

> If each person should follow his conscience, does that mean every individual can define for himself or herself what is right and wrong?

BIBLICAL TOUCHSTONES

I will place my law within them, and write it upon their hearts; I will be their God, and they shall be my people.

JEREMIAH 31:33

And for this reason we too give thanks to God unceasingly, that, in receiving the word of God from hearing us, you received not a human word but, as it truly is, the word of God, which is now at work in you who believe.

1 THESSALONIANS 2:13

Annunciation and Visitation

(C. 1230-1255)

Annunciation and Visitation, jamb statues of central doorway, west façade,
Reims Cathedral, Reims, France, c. 1230-1255.

Sacred Art and the Beatitudes
Conscience: God's Voice in Our Hearts

 Annunciation and Visitation (c. 1230-1255)

Directions: Take some time to quietly view and reflect on the art. Let yourself be inspired in any way that happens naturally. Then think about the questions below, and discuss them with your classmates.

Conversation Questions

1. What type of artwork do you see in this photograph? Where are these sculptures located?

2. How would you describe the expressions on the faces of these figures? Which is your favorite?

3. These sculptures tell the story of two of the Joyful Mysteries of the Rosary: the Annunciation (the two figures on the left) and the Visitation (the two figures on the right.) What happened at each of these events? Whom do the sculptures represent?

4. Read the story of the Visitation in Luke 1:39-45, and read the Magnificat in Luke 1:46-56. Based on these verses, what are some ways that the Blessed Virgin Mary and St. Elizabeth listen to God's voice in their hearts? How did they listen to God's voice in their hearts throughout their lives?

5. The figure to the far left is sometimes called the "Happy Angel." What is the connection between conscience and happiness?

6. We often think of a conscience as giving us feelings after we do something – guilt when we do something bad, for example. How can our conscience help us *before* we make a choice?

7. What are some things you can do to be able to hear and listen to God's voice in your own heart?

Materials

> Handout A: Conscience Cards

> Handout B: Well-Formed or Ill-Formed Conscience?

> Handout C: Examining Conscience According to the Beatitudes

Warm-Up   *15 minutes*

A. Preview, cut out, and distribute a set of cards from **Handout A: Conscience Cards**. Put students in pairs, and give each pair a set of cards. Instruct students to read the scenarios and decide if they would *act* the way the speaker wants to at the end of each scenario, or *avoid* acting that way. They should sort the scenario cards into two piles: ACT or AVOID. Encourage students to discuss among one another why they have chosen the particular category for each card.

B. When all pairs have had some time to sort a number of the cards, bring attention together to discuss the choices they made.

C. Transition the students to the discussion of "How do we know these are the right things to do?" Ask students what rules the Lord has given us to know the correct choice for each scenario. For example,

> Ten Commandments

> The Beatitudes

> The Corporal Works of Mercy

D. Share with students that in knowing and being familiar with these laws, we are able to judge situations and determine an action to be right or wrong. We call this ability to judge actions our conscience.

Activity I   *15 minutes*

A. Our conscience works as a voice in our hearts, guiding us out of love for God to know and choose what is good and avoid what is evil. Ask students to share situations where they have felt a voice in their heart prompting them to act in one way or another.

B. Read aloud Jeremiah 31:33: "I will place my law within them, and write it upon their hearts; I will be their God, and they shall be my people." Challenge students to recognize the correlation between the words of the prophet to the voice in our hearts. The voice in our hearts is the law of God, which He has written in our hearts. This is also where God speaks to us.

C. Introduce students to the importance of having a well-formed conscience. A conscience that is not formed according to what is good is dangerous and will lead us to sin. Have students imagine that their conscience told them it was okay to take a toy from the store without paying for it. It is hard to imagine that such an act would be, but when a conscience is not formed according to God's laws, it leads to sin.

D. Transition conversation to times when we may not know what the right (good) action is in a situation. In these times, we are not allowed to act, but instead must inform our conscience according to God's law. We do this through:

- the Church
- Sacred Scripture
- our family
- upright peers
- our priest and teachers

E. Occasionally our hearts may want to do what is wrong because evil is often the easier and more attractive choice. In these moments, we have to ask our hearts if what we are hearing is actually what the Church and Jesus' example teach us. Jesus wants us to follow Him so we can choose good and avoid evil.

Activity II   *20 minutes*

A. Divide students in groups of 3 or 4. Each group will receive two copies of **Handout B: Well-Formed or Ill-Formed Conscience?** Students will collaborate to brainstorm a scenario and write it out in two different ways — once to demonstrate a well-formed conscience, and a second time to show an ill-formed conscience.

B. Each group should then turn their scenario into a skit to present to the class. This can be done next class.

C. The audience of students will determine whether or not the character has a well-formed or ill-formed conscience, giving advice to the character to help him form his conscience and make the correct judgment of action. Encourage students to be specific by citing commandments, beatitudes, etc., in explaining their advice.

D. Depending on student maturity, you may wish to distribute **Handout C: Examining Conscience According to the Beatitudes** as a resource for students.

Day Two Lesson Plan

Materials

> Background Essay: Conscience: God's Voice in Our Hearts

> Handout D: Heroic Conscience

> Handout E: Church Wisdom on Conscience

> Handout F: Quiet versus Silence

Background/Homework

Have students read the **Background Essay: Conscience: God's Voice in Our Hearts** and answer the questions.

Warm-Up   *15 minutes*

A. As a large group, brainstorm a list of people from history who have followed their conscience for the sake of justice. Keep a list on the board. Refer to the saint biographies in lesson 12 for names to add to the ones students generate.

B. Distribute **Handout D: Heroic Conscience**. Have students write a brief reflection applying what they already know from history or religion classes.

C. Conduct a large group discussion to answer the questions:

> Why is it important for a conscience to be well-formed?

> Is it only people from the past who have faced challenges like this, or will people of our time have to face this struggle?

> What are some specific moral challenges our culture faces?

> What are some ways *you* can form your conscience in order to live a holy life?

Activity

A. Distribute **Handout E: Church Wisdom on Conscience**. Have students read the selections and discuss the questions. For homework, they should choose one quotation to respond to in a brief reflection paper. Note: You may wish to present the lesson on Aquinas and the Four Laws on page 6 as a lead-in to discussion on whether an individual is obliged to follow laws that his well-formed conscience tells him are unjust.

Wrap-Up

10 minutes

A. Distribute **Handout F: Quiet versus Silence**. Read it aloud together, and discuss habits students can practice to better hear God speaking to them. Witness to your students by sharing with them the ways you have made this type of activity a focus of your own life.

Conscience: God's Voice in Our Hearts ■ ■

Conscience makes man unique among all the creatures God has made. Conscience is a gift given to mankind through which God has an internal dialogue with us, guiding us to make judgments (or choices) that lead us to what is good for us and what will make us happy. Some people today think that "judging" is a bad thing. (Ironically, they have judged judging to be wrong.) But the truth is that we need to judge – to weigh our options and arrive at a decision – in order to make the right choices. We must judge right from wrong, good from evil, beautiful from distorted. Our conscience is one tool that helps us judge correctly.

What Is a Conscience?

Conscience is God's voice speaking to us at a specific time of decision. Saint Bonaventure teaches that "conscience is like God's herald and messenger; it does not command things on its own authority, but commands them as coming from God's authority, like a herald when he proclaims the edict of the king. This is why conscience has binding force" (*Veritatis Splendor*). The judgment of conscience makes known to us what we must do for a particular action.

Deep within each of us is a law that we did not create, a law that was written on our hearts by God and which we must obey to live the life God intended for us. This law acknowledges both our earthly obligations and our obligations to God. In other words, conscience, our internal law, tells us how to

Moses Receives the Tablets, João Zeferino da Costa

act justly toward God, other people in the world, and ourselves. Because conscience is an interior voice, it is necessary that we learn to listen to that voice. We have to be able to quiet down and turn off the external noise, to spend time in prayer and reflection to develop an internal "ear."

Judgments of Conscience

Judgments of conscience are not the same as decisions. You can make a decision to eat either pizza or a burger for dinner. Neither of these decisions has a moral implication. There is no need to consult one's conscience over a dinner choice of this variety. However, other choices clearly have moral implications. For example, choosing to drink or not drink at a party, or to drive or not drive home after drinking all involve moral judgments. In these moments, it is our obligation to listen to our consciences and allow God to speak to us the truth of the situation.

All actions have either good or bad results. Results, or consequences, are the outcomes of our actions. Conscience helps us to make a judgment only if we know there is a right and a wrong that we can choose between in a particular situation. There are some rules that always apply, no matter what the circumstances. You can never do evil so that good may come about. (The ends do not justify the means.) You should always follow the golden rule, and you must always be guided by charity and respect for your neighbor and his conscience (CCC 1789).

We have a moral obligation to follow our consciences. But, conscience must be formed throughout our lives. We do that in a variety of ways: reading Scripture, the *Catechism* and other Church teachings; listening to parents, teachers and the wisdom of other trusted leaders; listening to God's voice in prayer; and surrounding ourselves with friends that follow God's law and encourage us to do the same; our past moral choices also shape our conscience. So we can have a well-formed conscience, in which the voice of God rings clear and true, or a badly formed conscience, in which the voice of God is distorted and twisted by evil.

What Does Conscience Require?

Conscience requires three things: that we seek the truth, acknowledge the truth, and conform our actions to the truth. To do this, we must first know what the truth is. Jesus tells us that He is "the way, the truth, and the life." So, to live a conscientious life, we must conform our actions to Him. But, this is difficult to do in a world of temptations and misinformation. It is easy to seek the truth, a good. But, we become waylaid when we substitute a good for the Good, or a truth for the Truth. For example, having money is definitely better than being poor. Having money is a good. But, it is not the ultimate Good. And, when the acquisition of money becomes one's ultimate Good, then one ceases seeking the real ultimate Good, which is life with God.

Ananias restoring the sight of St. Paul, Pietro de Cortona

How Can the Beatitudes Form My Conscience?

We are responsible for seeking the truth and acting accordingly. However, even though we seek to be as conscientious as possible, we can still judge wrongly. It is possible for a person to develop an erroneous conscience by rejecting the natural law or the teachings of the Church, by allowing ourselves to be dominated by our passions for pleasure, vanity or power, or even by not bothering to find out how what is true and good. A conscience can also be badly formed by unwittingly adopting an action or attitude that is contrary to God's will if one was badly taught, if one does not believe or practice the Faith, if one is given bad example by others in authority.

The answer is to continually form our consciences according to the teaching of Christ, as taught in Scripture and in subsequent Church teaching. Scripture offers us two sets of guidelines for living a good life: the Ten Commandments and the Beatitudes. The Ten Commandments offer us a basic understanding of a right relationship with God, others, and ourselves. The Ten Commandments form our consciences to the basic rules of living justly.

The Beatitudes offer a fuller understanding of living a life in Christ. The Beatitudes invite us to live the Gospel and see Christ in everyone we encounter. This deeper explanation of the expectations of Christian living form our consciences to conform to the ultimate Good, which is life in Christ. The Beatitudes are not rules for living that we would have come up with on our own. The Beatitudes are divine and require grace. They respond to the desire for happiness that God has placed into the hearts of each person. For this reason, it is critical that prayer and reading of Scripture and Church teaching be a significant component in the development of conscience.

Conversation Questions

1. What is a conscience?
2. What are three rules that always apply when judging the morality of actions?
3. The modern world tends to call "judging" bad. What is the difference between being judgmental and judging? Why is judging essential for a moral life?
4. How can you form your conscience so that you are better able to listen to God when He speaks to you?

Conscience Cards

Teacher Note: These scenarios are arranged from simplest to most complex. Preview the cards and distribute the ones that are appropriate for your students.

Your mom made cookies for the neighbors. You see them when no one is else is around. They look good, and you want to take one.

You hear that a classmate is having a birthday party. You are not invited. Your heart begins to hurt. That classmate asks you to play at recess, but you want to tell him no.

Your mom packs you a healthy lunch each day. One day at school your friend brings cupcakes and gives one to everyone at your lunch table. Your friends eat a cupcake and throw their lunches away. You don't want to do that. You think it would be better to take a cupcake but save it for later.

Your mom tells you to clean up your room. You want to keep playing your favorite video game.

Your younger brother is having trouble learning how to ride his bike. You want to help him.

You got upset at your sister when she took the last piece of cake. You yell at her. Later you feel bad and want to apologize.

You forgot to complete your homework last night. Your friend offers to let you copy her answers, and you want to copy them.

You are working on an assignment in math class. It's hard, and you want to give up on it.

You were playing catch with your little brother in the house and you broke your mom's favorite glass vase. You want to clean it up so your mom won't notice you broke it.

The dog escaped from the yard after you left the gate open. Your dad asks if you were responsible for not shutting it. You want to tell him no so you don't get in trouble.

You were playing with two of your friends at recess. When one of them went to play on the swings, your other friend started saying bad things about her. You want to ask her to stop.

Your mom asks you to clean up your bedroom before you go over to your friend's house. You know it will take a really long time to clean up everything and it is already getting dark. You want to tell her that if you make your bed, that should be enough.

Your friends go out for pizza and don't invite you. You decide that you are going to have a pizza party the next weekend and you want to invite everyone except the friends who didn't invite you.

You are at the mall with two friends and they both start talking about going into one of the more popular stores and stealing something. They laugh about it as it would be fun. You want to tell them not to do it, and that stealing is wrong.

You are looking over your graded test and you notice that your teacher made a big mistake in your favor when she scored it. You know if you say something your grade will go down, but you feel like you should let your teacher know.

It's late at night and you are working on an essay for school. While looking up some information online, you see that someone has posted an essay on the exact same topic you are working on. You want to download that essay and turn it in as your own work.

Well-Formed or Ill-Formed Conscience?

Directions: Brainstorm a scenario and write it out in two different ways – one to demonstrate a well-formed conscience and the other to show an ill-formed conscience.

Dilemma/scenario:	
Choice of action with a well-formed conscience:	**Choice of action with a ill-formed conscience:**

HANDOUT C

Examining Conscience According to the Beatitudes

Directions: Read Jesus' teachings in the Beatitudes. The following is a resource you can use to examine your conscience with respect to these teachings. What other questions could you add?

1. **Blessed are the poor in spirit, for theirs is the kingdom of heaven.**

   Am I putting God's commandments ahead of my own preferences?

   Have I put my others' needs ahead of my own desires?

   Have I prayed to be open to discerning God's will for my life?

2. **Blessed are they who mourn, for they will be comforted.**

   Have I shared what I have, or even just my presence, with someone who is suffering?

   Do I go out of my way to show kindness to those who are different from me?

   Do I show compassion?

3. **Blessed are the meek, for they will inherit the land.**

   Have I borne wrongs patiently?

   Have I been gentle and kind?

   Have I striven to be humble, or have I been egotistical or boastful?

4. **Blessed are they who hunger and thirst for holiness, for they will be satisfied.**

   Do I spend time in prayer?

   Do I encourage others to seek a spiritual life?

   Do I work to build a culture of life?

5. Blessed are the merciful, for they will be shown mercy.

Am I forgiving and merciful?

Have I asked for someone's forgiveness?

Do I give others the benefit of the doubt, or am I harsh or judgmental?

6. Blessed are the pure of heart, for they will see God.

Do I put my faith and trust in God above all else?

Do I help younger siblings and friends stay focused on what's right?

Have I allowed a particular sin to distract me from God?

7. Blessed are the peacemakers, for they will be called children of God.

Do I look for ways to help friends and loved ones get along?

How often do I examine my conscience or go to confession?

How often am I aware of God's presence in my life?

8. Blessed are they who are persecuted for the sake of righteousness, for theirs is the kingdom of heaven.

Am I willing to follow my conscience even if it means being seen as different?

Have I been a witness to the love of Jesus Christ?

How often do I help those who are the least among us, the most vulnerable?

Heroic Conscience

St. Thomas More, Bl. Mother Teresa, Dorothy Day, St. Maximilian Kolbe, Bl. Miguel Pro. What do these people have in common?

St. John Paul II, in his encyclical *Evangelium Vitae*, discussed the culture of death and talked about the "moral conscience of society." When practices such as contraception, abortion, unchecked poverty, racism, human trafficking, or euthanasia become commonplace, it is possible for an entire culture to blur the lines between what is immoral and what is acceptable. In this instance, acceptance of these acts can permeate a culture and be taught to future generations. Yet, even in these times, God is still speaking truth. Those who are open to hearing His Word will be inspired to rise up in heroic ways to confront the evil that they see.

> › **Think of a person you know (a famous person or a personal acquaintance) who is heroic in the face of injustice. What makes that person heroic? How is that person following his or her conscience? What effect has that person had on you, and on the culture?**

Church Wisdom on Conscience

Directions: Read the following selections and discuss the questions below. Finally, choose one quotation to respond to in a brief reflection paper.

Proverbs 3:5-6

Trust in the LORD with all your heart,
on your own intelligence do not rely;
In all your ways be mindful of him,
and he will make straight your paths.

Psalm 119:104-106

Through your precepts I gain understanding;
therefore I hate all false ways.
Your word is a lamp for my feet,
a light for my path.
I make a solemn vow
to observe your righteous judgments.

St. Peter and St. Paul, Jusepe de Ribera

2 Timothy 1:13-14

Take as your norm the sound words that you heard from me, in the faith and love that are in Christ Jesus.

Guard this rich trust with the help of the Holy Spirit that dwells within us.

1 Thessalonians 2:13

And for this reason we too give thanks to God unceasingly, that, in receiving the word of God from hearing us, you received not a human word but, as it truly is, the word of God, which is now at work in you who believe.

John Henry Cardinal Newman

[Conscience] is a messenger of Him, who, both in nature and in grace, speaks to us behind a veil, and teaches and rules us by his representatives. Conscience is the aboriginal Vicar of Christ.

CCC 1778

In all he says and does, man is obliged to follow faithfully what he knows to be just and right.

Gaudium et Spes 16

Deep within their consciences men and women discover a law which they have not laid upon themselves and which they must obey. Its voice, ever calling them to love and to do what is good and to avoid evil, tells them inwardly at the right moment: do this, shun that. For they have in their hearts a law inscribed by God. Their dignity rests in observing this law, and by it they will be judged. Their conscience is people's most secret core, and their sanctuary. There they are alone with God whose voice echoes in their depths. By conscience, in a wonderful way, that law is made known which is fulfilled in the love of God and of one's neighbor.

1. Since we are obliged to follow the certain judgments of our consciences, why is a well-formed conscience so important to a moral life?

2. Do you think the picture of conscience painted by these quotations matches up with what most people think a conscience is? Why or why not?

3. How can the Word of God be "at work" within us? What can we do to ensure we are open to this Word?

4. Which of the quotations above most speaks to you? Write a short reflection in response to it.

Quiet versus Silence

The formation of conscience requires us to take the time to listen to the voice of God, not only in the moment of decision-making, but throughout our lives. By developing a habit of stillness, we can come to hear God's voice and recognize it clearly. This allows to not only hear but to listen to God's command at critical moments of our lives, including times when we are faced with difficult choices. Even if we are quiet externally, there might be a running dialogue inside us. Silence, on the other hand, is a stillness that allows God to speak and us to hear.

What are some ways habits that we can practice that will allow us to better hear God speaking to us?

> Unplug from the constant noise and distraction of everyday life. Today, we are in constant contact through our electronic devices. Take a few minutes away each day to sit in stillness and silence.

> Go to adoration. Spend time in the presence of God.

> Read Scripture for inspiration, then meditate on what you have read. Begin with the biblical touchstones in this lesson.

> Pray the Rosary. Meditate on the mysteries of the life of Jesus.

> Take a walk in nature, noticing the wonder of God's creation.

> Add your own ideas:

_____

_____

_____

_____

Answer Key

Sacred Art and the Beatitudes: Conscience

1. Sculptures; Reims Cathedral, France

2. Accept reasoned answers.

3. At the Annunciation (the two figures on the left), the Archangel Gabriel announced to the Virgin Mary that she would be the mother of Jesus and Mary consented to this mission. At the Visitation (the two figures on the right), Mary visited her cousin St. Elizabeth, who was pregnant with St. John the Baptist. Both Elizabeth and her baby immediately knew and rejoiced that the Lord was with Mary.

4. They both trust in God and make decisions conformed to His will.

5. One of God's greatest gifts to us is our consciences – He speaks directly to us through our consciences, and allows us to freely make the moral judgments and choices that will make us happy.

6. Our conscience can help us lead a holy life if we conform it to Church teaching and listen to it before we act.

7. Accept reasoned answers.

Background Essay

1. Your conscience judges whether actions are right or wrong. God offers to speak to you in your conscience, if you are open to hearing Him.

2. You can never do evil so that good may result; you must always follow the golden rule, and you must always be guided by charity toward your neighbor and respect for his conscience.

3. Being judgmental means being overly critical. It is not the same thing as judgment. Judging is essential to a moral life because right and wrong exist. We must decide whether actions are right or wrong. God has given us free will and a conscience in order that we may do these things with His help.

4. By learning seeking the truth, acknowledging it and confirming oneself to it. We can inform our consciences through Sacred Scripture, the Church, our parents, upright peers, our priests, and our teachers.

Handout D: Church Wisdom on Conscience

1. Because a well-formed conscience will help us to follow God's commands and live a holy life. It will help us avoid sin.

2. Probably not. The world tends to think of a conscience as an individual's preferences, rather than a truth God has written on our hearts to help us follow Him.

3. God's Word can work within us every day as we go through life, making moral judgments about how to conduct ourselves and treat others. Ideas for being open to discerning God's will and forming our consciences can be found on **Handout F**.

4. Accept reasoned answers.

Vocation: The Universal Call to Holiness

Overview

Derived from the Latin *vocare*, "to call," vocation extends beyond the specific call to the priesthood. This discussion-based lesson uses Renaissance and Baroque art and the *Catechism of the Catholic Church* to highlight the proper understanding of vocation. Finally, the lesson offers an interview project that puts students in touch with the various manifestations of God's call to the holy life.

Grade Levels

 MS  HS

Time

One fifty-minute class

Connection to the Catechism

› CCC 2013

› CCC 2337

› CCC 2544–2546

Essential Questions

› How do I fit in to God's plan to save the world?

› What is a holy life?

› How can I be holy?

BIBLICAL TOUCHSTONES

O God, you are my God—
it is you I seek!
For you my body yearns;
for you my soul thirsts,
In a land parched, lifeless,
and without water.

PSALM 63:2

From now on the crown of righteousness awaits me, which the Lord, the just judge, will award to me on that day, and not only to me, but to all who have longed for his appearance.

2 TIMOTHY 4:8

The Calling of St. Matthew
BY CARAVAGGIO (C. 1599-1600)

Caravaggio, *The Calling of St. Matthew*, c. 1599-1600, oil on canvas.
Contarelli Chapel, Church of San Luigi dei Francesi.

Sacred Art and the Beatitudes
Vocation: The Universal Call to Holiness

The Calling of St. Matthew, *by Caravaggio* (c. 1599-1600)

Directions: Take some time to quietly view and reflect on the art. Let yourself be inspired in any way that happens naturally. Then think about the questions below, and discuss them with your classmates.

Conversation Questions

1. Whom do you see in this painting, and what appears to be happening?

2. What do you notice about the colors the artist chose? How does the light look? Where is it coming from?

3. What are some feelings that this painting inspires in you?

4. Who do you think is St. Matthew in this painting? Which figure is Jesus?

5. Jesus is the man to the far right pointing at St. Matthew (who is pointing at himself, appearing to say "Who, me?"). The older man standing next to Jesus is St. Peter. Why is St. Peter imitating Jesus?

6. Read Luke 5:27-28. How does this painting enhance your understanding of these verses?

7. If you were a figure in this painting, who would you be?

8. In your own life, are you listening for God's call? What can you do to listen to it more carefully?

Lesson Plan

Materials

- *Catechism of the Catholic Church*
- Holy Bible
- The Creation of Adam (page 2)
- Teacher Resource: Art Discussion Form
- Handout A: Worksheet on the Evangelical Counsels
- Handout B: Interview Project

Warm-Up

25 minutes

A. Show *The Calling of St. Matthew* to students. Ask them to look at this masterpiece and to write down who they think is St. Matthew and why.

Note: *The discussion will draw out the personal nature of a call from God. While God calls all to a holy life, that holy life and call take unique forms. The call is a moment of grace as represented by the light shining from above. Some, however, are not predisposed to hearing God's call. Some of the figures in Caravaggio's work represent the kinds of obstacles to the faithful for recognizing God's call. It is Christ who calls, but often the call comes mediated through people in our lives, especially through the Church, represented by the figure of St. Peter who imitates Christ in Caravaggio's work. The introduction of* The Creation of Adam *will lead to conclusions about our vocation having its foundation in God's Providence and the initial creation of man in the beginning.*

B. Begin discussion with easy questions that everyone can answer with concrete information. From the easier, opening questions, you can move the discussion toward more abstract concepts about meaning and symbolism.

C. Use **Teacher Resource: Art Discussion Form** to guide and record discussion. The left column includes the points that you intend to cover by the discussion. The three empty spaces provide space for significant points made in the discussion but not intended. Discussions will go in unexpected directions. Use the open space on the chart to record key insights so you can assess them on a later test, for example, in an essay question.

D. Read (or ask a student to read aloud) Luke 5:27-28 about the call of Levi, Matthew's original name before being called by Jesus. Ask them to identify St. Matthew and explain their reasoning. How would you describe St. Matthew's reaction? Why is he reacting this way? *St. Matthew is the older gentleman, sitting at the table, pointing to himself as if to say, "Who? Me?"*

E. Then ask them to identify Jesus Christ. *Jesus Christ is the one standing on the right side, whose face we can mostly see, pointing to Levi.*

F. Ask what Caravaggio has done to draw our attention to St. Matthew. *You will notice many straight lines, called "diagonals" in artistic terms, which point to St. Matthew. The beam of light from the right, three pointed fingers, the sword under the table, and even many of the arms and legs of the figures present point to St. Matthew. Jesus' call is to him and to him alone.*

G. How is everyone else reacting? What about the figures at the left side of the table? *They don't even notice Jesus. Why? Counting money and distracted with earthly concerns, they are ill-disposed to hear God's call. Rhetorically, you can ask the students about their disposition to hear God's call.*

H. Pose the questions: Do you notice God's call or are you too distracted? How does one improve their chances of hearing God's call? *The figures sitting at the right side of the table notice the call and are even eager to respond, but this particular call is not for them. What does this suggest about the nature of a vocation? Our individual calls vary, and our desire should be to fulfill God's call for us, not God's call for someone else. Envy has no place in responding to the call to holiness.*

I. Who is the bearded figure on the right side, standing in front of Jesus, imitating His pointing? *This is a difficult question and students are unlikely to guess correctly. After a few guesses, you can tell them that it's St. Peter.*

J. Why is St. Peter imitating Jesus? *Because he is the Pope, the "Vicar" of Christ, who visibly represents on Earth the invisible Christ. We do not see much of his face because it's not so much St. Peter and his identity that matter, or Pope Francis or any other pope, but the papal office as Christ's vicar. Notice that St. Peter stands between Christ and us, the viewers. He mediates between Christ and the living faithful.*

K. How does this mediation play into vocation? *You hope that students will be able to point out that God's will can be known to us through various people in our lives (the Magisterium, priests, parents, teachers, et al.).*

L. Now introduce the second painting, Michelangelo's *The Creation of Adam* on page 2 of this guide. Ask the students what similarity they see between the two works.

Some students will very likely notice (with much surprise) that Adam's hand in Michelangelo's work is the same as Christ's hand in The Calling of St. Matthew.

A. Why? Why does Caravaggio want the viewer to think of Creation in his piece on Matthew's calling? What does Creation have to do with vocation?

The answer to this question is complex and multi-layered. The students will provide some profound and creative insights. Jesus Christ is the "New Adam." He exemplifies the holy life to which all are called and that Adam failed to fulfill. Christ says to Levi, "Follow me," but He says to all, "Follow me." Here, though, the universal call is particularized in an individual, personal way. We are all called to holiness in the moment of creation—Adam representing all mankind—and God knows and wills from our collective inception how we are to fulfill His call uniquely. Thus, we see Christ calling only Levi, to be Matthew, in that graced moment captured in the painting, and thus we can imagine Christ calling "only me" somehow in life, if we have ears to hear. Further, in Caravaggio's work Jesus possesses the hand of Adam but takes the side of God, that is, the right side of the painting. In doing this, Caravaggio presents the two natures of Christ Jesus, that He is true God and true man. The painting captures multiple truths at once about the nature of God and the nature of man and how the call to holiness manifests universally and in single instances. What is important overall is the realization that God purposefully and personally designed an individual call for each and every one of us, fitted into salvation history and fulfilled in the life of Christ, who leads, teaches, loves and informs us. "Before I formed you in the womb I knew you, before you were born I dedicated you." (Jeremiah 1:5)

Activity

25 minutes

A. Distribute **Handout A: Worksheet on the Evangelical Counsels**. Students may work individually or in small groups. Students should write out definitions, and determine how Christ (first column), religious (second column), lay people (third column), and they themselves (fourth column) might exemplify the three counsels of poverty, obedience and chastity. Students can find good definitions in the glossary of the *Catechism of Catholic Church*.

Extension Option

A. Using **Handout B: Interview Project**, give students the task of interviewing a person (priest, religious, or lay) whom they consider to be striving to live a holy life. The interview should include the person's own explanation of "vocation" and his or her personal testimony and experience in having been called to holiness and a particular state of life. After the interviews, students should write a one-page summary to present to the class. The typically beautiful stories associated with conversions and vocations can have a lasting and instructive effect.

Vocation

Commonly when Catholics think of vocations they think strictly of priests and nuns. In other words, the word is associated strictly with receiving the sacrament of holy orders or making religious vows. But the word "vocation" involves everyone baptized into Christ. "Vocation" is not for the chosen few but for everyone who is in the Church.

It is true that priests and religious provide the easiest to recognize examples of the holy life to which the Lord Jesus calls us all. When we see a priest, we think of God. Priests and religious act as signs to remind all people of their supernatural destiny and their call to holiness. In and of itself, the call to religious life is an excellent and true example of the way God calls individuals to serve His greater purpose. But before arriving to a "state of life" in the Church like the priesthood or religious life, we are called by the Lord to live our general vocation to holiness. As the Second Vatican Council teaches, the first vocation of every Christian is to follow Jesus in the universal call to holiness. God calls each and every one of us to serve Him, and He has given us all our own unique talents and capabilities to do so.

What Is a Vocation?

Derived from the Latin *vocare*, which means "to call," vocation in a general sense to be like God: "Be holy for I am holy" and "Be holy as your Father is holy." We answer that call to holiness by becoming a member of

Medieval sculpture of the Virgin Mary with the Christ Child (AMzPhoto / Shutterstock.com)

Christ (entering the Church) and following Him. However, Our Divine Maker has made each person unique and so summons us personally to a particular state of life, and in a specific way to fulfill His will. In other words, our universal vocation leads to our particular vocation, to a particular state of life in the Church. The three states of life in the Church are married life, the priesthood and consecrated life (also called "religious life"). Our greatest happiness lies in discovering our particular vocation in Christ, that state of life for which He made us to help Him in His work of saving the world.

A particular state of life in the Church is about love and being united to Jesus. Therefore, a particular vocation will involve taking lifelong vows of some sort. For the married person they are the vows of holy matrimony. For the priest they are the promises he makes at ordination and for the consecrated person they are the vows of the evangelical counsels of poverty, chastity and obedience. Thus, the "single life" means a person who has consecrated his or her life to Christ through public or private vows and lives out that consecration in the world, or it means a person who is still discerning their vocation. The Lord Jesus always calls us to a permanent state of life in the Church.

In this regard, it is good to note the dignity of every human person, no matter his particular state of life in the Church. All are called to be holy according to their state of life, and so no one individual purpose is better compared to another. As St. Catherine of Siena says, "Be who God meant you to be and you will set the world on fire." The saints give many examples of just how rich and varied the call to holiness is among the members of the Church.

"You did not choose me, but I chose you" –John 15:16

Before we can answer God's call to be who He wants us to be, we must have the right understanding of happiness. Often we don't know what will really make us happy. Our vision is clouded by Original Sin. The world tells us that passing pleasures, worldly success, or being with the "right person" will make us happy. Our Lord, who always followed the will of the Father, helps us see that happiness doesn't come from following our own ideas, but from seeking to do the Father's will.

The next step is to know that God created you for a specific mission in this world. There is no one else like you; you are totally unique. You were created out of love, you are part of His mission to save the world. Accept His love and His choice for you. When we hand over our wills to Him, we allow Him to make us happy and fulfilled.

And of course, you must be listening for and praying to discern that call. It might not come the way you expect or hope! Not every call includes a miraculous healing, a burning bush, a bolt of lightning, or a fall from a horse and a period of literal, physical blindness as it meant for St. Paul. Rather, sometimes the form of one's vocation is not flashy at all but humble. Nevertheless, the call God gives to each one of us is the right one. Make yourself available to God by going to Him in adoration before the Blessed Sacrament, in Holy Mass, and confession. Pray the Rosary, and be inspired by the lives of the saints.

God calls you, too. If you pray to understand that call, you will be on the path to happiness in this life and supreme joy in the next.

Worksheet on the Evangelical Counsels ▪ ■

Directions: Write out the definitions for the three evangelical counsels. Then determine ways in which Christ, priests and religious, lay people, and yourself exemplify poverty, obedience, and chastity, and fill in the rest of the chart.

Evangelical Counsel	Christ	Priests and Religious	Lay People	You
Poverty				
Obedience				
Chastity				

Define evangelical counsels:

Interview Project

Personally interview a person (priest, religious, or lay — ***not your religion teacher***) whom you consider to be striving to live a holy life. You should carefully record questions and answers. The interview should include the person's own explanation of "vocation" and his or her personal testimony and experience in having been called to holiness and a particular state of life. Produce a one-page report of the interview to present to the class and turn in for a grade.

Focus questions

1. How do you define "vocation"?
2. Would you say that everyone has a vocation, or only people who receive holy orders or get married?
3. If God calls everyone, how should everyone respond?
4. How does considering a vocation affect my life?
5. What is your vocation story? When did you ever first hear "the call"? Was it life-changing and something you realized immediately, or did you consider your life path for a long time?
6. Who were instrumental or influential figures that helped you to follow your call?
7. Who is your favorite saint, and why?
8. What is your advice to someone who thinks he or she may have a call to the priesthood or religious life?

Art Discussion Form

Who is St. Matthew? How is everyone responding? What obstacles prevent hearing God's call?	Student Insights
› God's call is both personal and universal. All are called to holiness. But we cooperate in God's plan in unique ways, specific to us as individuals. › Worldly distractions can keep us from hearing God's call. › The evangelical counsels of poverty, obedience, and chastity help us to hear God's voice and fulfill our vocation.	
Why is St. Peter in the painting? What is he doing?	**Student Insights**
› St. Peter symbolizes both the Pope and the visible Church. › God's will is often mediated through various people and institutions in our lives, including the Magisterium, priests, parents, and teachers.	
Why is it important to link Creation to the idea of vocation? How do these paintings connect the two ideas, that God created all of us, and that God calls each of us?	**Student Insights**
› Since the beginning, God has had a plan for us and made us in His image and likeness for holiness and a purpose. › God's call manifests itself especially through Christ (and others who are Christ-like); He was sent to lead us out of sin. We cannot return of our own volition. › As in the painting, we are charged to learn to hear His voice and be drawn back to the Father, away from worldly distractions.	

Answer Key

Sacred Art and the Beatitudes: Vocation

1. A group of men are seated at a table. A bearded man standing on the right side of the painting is pointing at one of the men at the table. Another man just in front of him seems to be imitating his gesture.

2. Accept reasoned answers.

3. Accept reasoned answers.

4. Accept reasoned answers, but let students know that it is generally agreed that St. Matthew is the man pointing at himself as if to say, "Who? Me?" The pointing man on the right is Jesus.

5. St. Peter was the first Pope. The Pope is the vicar of Christ, or the visible representative of Christ on Earth.

6-8. Accept reasoned answers.

Handout B: Worksheet on the Evangelical Counsels

These definitions have come from the glossary of the *Catechism of the Catholic Church*. The rest of the spaces provide examples of answers but do not exhaust all possible correct answers.

Ecumenical Counsel	Christ	Priests and Religious	Lay People	You
Poverty: Poverty is one of the three evangelical counsels whose public profession in the Church is a constitutive element of consecrated life (915). Poverty of spirit signifies detachment from worldly things and voluntary humility (2544–2546).	Humbled Himself, taking the form of a slave and dying on a cross; born in humble stable among animals; lived a simple, austere life without many possessions	Vow of poverty; renounces earthly possessions entirely and all private property; community holds property in common	Detachment from worldly goods; almsgiving; tithing	

Ecumenical Counsel	Christ	Priests and Religious	Lay People	You
Obedience: The submission to the authority of God which requires everyone to obey the divine law...as an evangelical counsel, the faithful may profess a vow of obedience; a public vow of obedience, accepted by Church authority	Obedient until death, fulfilling the Father's will; Jesus prays in the Garden of Gethsemane (Mark 14:36).	Vow of obedience; obedience to superiors, abbot or bishop	Obedience to parents; obedience to the state; obedience to Church law; obedience to legitimate authority	
Chastity: The moral virtue which, under the cardinal virtue of temperance, provides for the successful integration of sexuality within the person leading to the inner unity of the bodily and spiritual being (2337).	Jesus never married, and His entire life exemplified pureness of heart and intention.	Celibacy; forgoes the good of marriage for the sake of the Kingdom.	Chastity and purity; fasting and mortification	

Define Evangelical Counsels:

In general, the teachings of the New Law given by Jesus to His disciples which lead to the perfection of Christian life. In the New Law, the precepts are intended to remove whatever is incompatible with charity; the evangelical counsels are to remove whatever might hinder the development of charity, even if not contrary to it (1973). The public profession of the evangelical counsels of poverty, chastity, and obedience is a constitutive element of the state of consecrated life in the Church (915).

Teacher Notes

Vocation: What Is God Calling Me to Do?

LESSON OVERVIEW

Overview

In this lesson, students will explore the concepts of holiness and vocation. Holiness means living like the Lord lives – in love. Vocations, or calls to various states of life, are not something only received by a select few. Rather, God calls each and every one of us to be holy. Using the saints as their first examples, students will identify how all individuals can receive special gifts and talents from God and can live out their vocation. Finally they will determine their unique gifts and talents that enable them to offer love to the world.

Connection to the Catechism

- › CCC 2012-2013
- › CCC 2016

Essential Questions

- › What is holiness?
- › What is a vocation? Don't only certain special people receive a call from God?
- › How specifically might God be calling *me* to live a holy life?

Grade Level

 ES

Time

One fifty-minute class

Before I formed you in the womb I knew you, before you were born I dedicated you.

JEREMIAH 1:5

Be perfect as your heavenly Father is perfect.

MATTHEW 5:48

69

Lesson Plan

Student Materials

- Saint cards (pages 209-242)
- Handout A: Gifts and Talents
- Handout B: My Family's Gifts and Talents

Warm-Up
20 minutes

A. Before class, prepare enough copies of **Handout A: Gifts and Talents** for each student to be able to complete four charts. Select three saints from the cards on pages 209-242. Pass out copies of the cards or read the stories aloud.

B. Discussing one saint at a time, ask the children to identify the saint's interests, gifts, and talents. Engage students in brainstorming some of the different ways the person lived out these interests and used his gifts to serve those around him. Fill in **Handout A** throughout the discussion.

C. Repeat the same steps for two more saints.

Activity
30 minutes

A. Ask children what all of these men and women have in common. Students' answers will vary, but should follow the theme that all of them had different interests and talents and used them to serve others in various ways.

B. Also guide students to ponder the notion of holiness. What does it mean to be holy? These individuals are saints living in heaven, so we know they are holy, but what specifically is evidence of their holiness being lived out while on Earth?

C. Share with students the definition of holiness from Jesus in the Gospel of St. Matthew: "Be perfect, as your heavenly Father is perfect." Does this mean we must be perfect and cannot make mistakes or fail at any time? No, of course not! Our heavenly Father is Love, so to be perfect as He is means we must love as He does. We must love not only when it is easy to love, but even more so when it is very hard to give our love. Holiness is about love.

D. Then pose the question: Are only certain, special people called to holiness? No! In the Gospel, Jesus tells *all* of us that we shall be perfect as our heavenly Father is perfect. Discuss how our adoption as sons and daughters of God calls us to holiness, and the grace we receive as an inheritance makes us able to become saints. Although everyone is called to holiness, we are created to love in our own special way, this is our vocation. When we look at our gifts and the desires God has given us, we are able to determine how God created us to love.

E. Children often think that they have to wait until they are adults to live their vocation, but ask them: Are we to live a holy life now, as children? Yes! Each day we are to use our gifts, talents and opportunities to love others. Have students pair and share ways they give love at home, as well as at school. Reiterate that this is living the holiness they are called to now.

F. Their current vocation is to be a daughter/son, sibling, and a student. In the future, some of us will be called to be great mothers and fathers, others of us will be called to serve the poor across the world, others of us will be called to be consecrated only to God by being priests, brothers, and sisters. Each is a different road to holiness, based on the gifts and desires that God gives to each person.

G. From the moment we are created, God gives us special gifts and talents to carry out His mission of love on Earth in our own unique way. We saw this in the saints we discussed earlier. Their acts of service brought love to others. Brainstorm the different concrete acts of love shown and how ultimately each act was an act of love for God. Compare the different ages, as well as the states in life of each of the saints, emphasizing that holiness is something that we are called to live to the fullest no matter our age or our state in life.

H. Ask students to think of an adult they know who is a great inspiration and an example of holiness. Each student may record the name of the person at the top of Handout A. Encourage students to list concrete examples of the person's gifts and talents and how they use them. Note: *In some cases it may be helpful for them to identify the right column first and fill in the gifts and talents they use second, as it may come easier for the children to identify the concrete actions before connecting them to a more abstract gift or talent.*

I. Call on a few students to share their recorded thoughts with the class. Pose the question, "How do these actions share love with God?" and engage students in discussion to clarify that in loving our neighbor, we are loving God who dwells in everyone. Also talk about how this person is still living and is not yet in heaven. Are we able to see and witness their holiness? Is this person striving to be perfect as our heavenly Father is perfect? What is his or her current state of life? Can holiness be lived out in every state of life?

Wrap-Up

A. Using a blank copy of **Handout A**, have students complete the chart using themselves as the person to analyze. Students should identify their own strengths, gifts, and desires and brainstorm different ways they can use them to serve others both now and in the future

Homework

Send home **Handout B: My Family's Gifts and Talents** with the following note:

Dear parents,

Your child has learned about the inheritance we receive at Baptism as sons and daughters of God, and our call to holiness. We brainstormed gifts and talents God has given us. We also identified various ways we are able to use our gifts to love and serve Him and the world. Assist your child in filling out the provided handout on discovering your family's gifts. Engage in conversation about how and when you discovered these gifts, as well as how you use them to love and serve others.

Discuss with your child the possible ways the Lord could be calling them to use his/her own gifts to love in an even greater way. Pray with your child asking the Lord to continue to guide your child in uncovering his/her greater vocation to love and his/her path to living a holy life.

Bulletin Board Extension

Have students pick a saint for which a card is not provided in this guide. They should use their textbook or other classroom resources to create a new, one-sided saint card with a photo and some key information on the front. Then have students make a one-sided "saint card" for themselves, listing several ways they can use their gifts and talents to serve others, and to serve the Lord. Display all the cards together on a Bulletin Board entitled, "We are all called to be saints." Write the Pope Francis quote from **Handout B** in the center:

"To be a saint is not a privilege of a few ... All of us in baptism have the inheritance of being able to become saints. Sanctity is a vocation for everyone."
— Pope Francis

Gifts and Talents

◼

Directions: Fill in the person's name at the top. Then complete the chart with a list of the gifts and talents God has given to this person, and how he or she used or uses those talents to serve God.

Name: _____

Gift/Talent	How s/he uses it to serve God

My Family's Gifts and Talents

■

Directions: Together with a parent or guardian, complete the chart. Talk about how and when your parent/guardian discovered these gifts, as well as how he or she uses them to love and serve others. Discuss the possible ways the Lord could be calling you to use your gifts to love in an even greater way. Pray together asking the Lord to continue to guide you in uncovering a greater vocation to love and your path to living a holy life.

> "To be a saint is not a privilege of a few ... all of us in baptism have the inheritance of being able to become saints. Sanctity is a vocation for everyone." — Pope Francis

Name: _____

Gift/Talent	How s/he uses it to serve God

On the back of this page, draw a picture of you and your family serving God together.

The Passions in the Christian Life

Overview

We are often told "go with your heart" or "if it feels good, do it." Such attitudes are not real or true and have been quite destructive in many ways. Both classical wisdom and the Fathers of the Church gave a definite picture of how "the passions" properly fit into a well-lived life. In this lesson students will come to understand the proper role of feelings as they grow to emotional maturity.

Connection to the Catechism

> CCC 1762-1775

Essential Questions

> What are the passions?

> Are feelings good or bad?

> How can our feelings help us get to heaven?

Grade Levels

■ ES   ■ MS   ■ HS

Time

One fifty-minute class

BIBLICAL TOUCHSTONES

More tortuous than anything is the human heart, beyond remedy; who can understand it? I, the LORD, explore the mind and test the heart, giving to all according to their ways, according to the fruit of their deeds.

JEREMIAH 17:9-10

But put on the Lord Jesus Christ, and make no provision for the desires of the flesh.

ROMANS 13:14

The Agony in the Garden
BY DOMÍNIKOS THEOTOKÓPOULOS (C. 1610-1612)

Domínikos Theotokópoulos (El Greco), *The Agony in the Garden* (c. 1610-1612),
Budapest Museum of Fine Arts.

Sacred Art and the Beatitudes
Passions in the Christian Life

 The Agony in the Garden, *by Domínikos Theotokópoulos (c. 1610-1612)*

Directions: Take some time to quietly view and reflect on the art. Let yourself be inspired in any way that happens naturally. Then think about the questions below, and discuss them with your classmates.

Conversation Questions

1. When you look at this painting, what do you first notice? What is your favorite part?

2. Do the figures in this painting look realistic? If not, how would you describe the way they look? How do the unreal shapes add to the painting's expressiveness?

3. Who are the people in this painting? What sorrowful mystery of the Rosary is depicted here?

4. Read Matthew 26:36-46 and Luke 22:39-46. How does this painting help you understand these verses?

5. What feelings does Jesus describe having in this Gospel passage? What other feelings do you think He might have experienced during this time? Why?

6. What do the Gospels tell us that Peter, James, and John were feeling?

7. What do this painting and the Gospel story of the Agony in the Garden teach us about how we should understand our feelings?

Lesson Plan

Materials

> Background Essay: The Passions in the Christian Life

> Handout A: What Our Lord Saw from the Cross

> Handout B: Catholic Wisdom on Feelings

> Handout C: Feelings Scenarios

Background/Homework

Have students read the **Background Essay: The Passions in the Christian Life** and answer the questions.

Warm-Up   *10 minutes*

A. Project an image the painting on **Handout A: What Our Savior Saw from the Cross**. Discuss the following questions as a large group.

> Whom do you see in this painting?
> *St. Mary of Magdala, St. John, the Blessed Virgin, a Roman centurion, many others.*

> From whose point of view are we seeing this scene? How do you know?
> *We see the scene from the perspective of Jesus Christ, as He hangs on the Cross. We can even see His feet at the bottom of the Cross.*

> What experience do you think the artist was trying to give his viewer with this painting?
> *By putting the viewer in Jesus' position, the artist might have been trying to help us empathize with the suffering of Jesus Christ during His Passion. He might have been trying to help us feel just a tiny bit of what Jesus felt.*

B. Ask students if the painting does a good job of allowing us to empathize in a small way with Jesus' suffering. What do you think He likely felt? [Pain, humiliation, fear, sorrow, and so forth]

C. Draw students' attention to the fact that Jesus had a human nature, and He had feelings.

D. If Jesus did something, He made it new, and He made it good. Our feelings are natural and in themselves are neither good nor bad. But we can allow our feelings to help us make good choices, or allow them to incline us toward sin. What we do with our feelings and how we allow them to figure into our actions can make the difference between upright actions and sin.

Activity

30 minutes

A. Write on the board: *"The human person is ordered to beatitude by his deliberate acts: the passions or feelings he experiences can dispose him to it and contribute to it."* (CCC 1762) Ask students to work in pairs to restate this fact in their own words.

B. Reconvene the class and have students share their paraphrases. Decide on the best one and write it on the board. It should say something like "We are made to go to heaven, and our feelings can help get us there."

C. Cut out and distribute strips from **Handout B: Catholic Wisdom on Feelings**. Give each student 1-3 strips. Note: *The strips on this Handout are arranged from the simplest statements to the most complex; use the strips that are most appropriate for the students' reading level and maturity. You could also give different strips to different students to provide differentiation.*

D. Have students paraphrase the statement(s) on their strip(s) on the back of the paper. Walk around the room and spot check for understanding.

E. Preview the scenarios on **Handout C: Feelings Scenarios** and decide which to present. You may wish to add your own original scenarios based on student interests. Divide the class into as many sections or teams as you will have scenarios.

F. Read aloud one scenario from **Handout C**. Ask the students in Team 1 to respond to the questions, and apply at least one statement from **Handout B** in support of their answer. Students on the other team(s) should try to predict the response on their own notepaper. Continue with the remaining teams/scenarios.

Wrap-Up

10 minutes

A. Discuss with students how feelings can help us get to heaven by helping us know what is good and what is bad. With the help of grace and a well-formed conscience, we can know instinctively that an action is good or bad and our feelings will confirm that understanding. Assuming we have a well-formed conscience, bad actions make us feel sad, guilty, ashamed, and so forth, while good actions make us feel happy, content, fulfilled, and so forth The goal in forming our consciences is to dispose ourselves toward what is good, beautiful, and true. Doing good should and will make us happy. When our conscience is well-formed and we strive to grow closer to Christ, we are more naturally drawn to what is good. Only what is good can be truly loved.

Extension Options

A. Have students compose their own scenarios that demonstrate the role of feelings in good or bad decision-making. They should share with the class next time, discussing questions similar to those on **Handout C**.

B. Have students watch the sports movie, "When the Game Stands Tall" (PG) starring Jim Caviezel. Direct them to write a reflection that clearly shows the place of feelings in a moral life.

Bulletin Board Option

Create a bulletin board that visually depicts the proper role of feelings using original student art and strips from **Handout B**.

> - Have students create their own artwork in the style of El Greco. They should select a moment from a favorite book, TV show, or film, when a character faces an emotional decision and depict the feelings of that moment.

> - What decision or testing point did the character face?

> - Did the character rule his/her emotions with reason, or was he/she overcome by emotion?

> - Students' composition, color, style, and so forth should clearly show whether the moment was one of emotional turmoil, or peace.

> - Post examples on the bulletin board with good decisions by characters on one side and bad decisions on the other, and discuss the contrast.

> - Further decorate the bulletin board with strips from **Handout B**.

Passions in the Christian Life

"The Passions," as they are called in classical and Church language, are better known now as "feelings." The *Catechism* describes them together as our "sensitive appetite." The principal passions are love and hatred, desire and fear, joy, sadness, and anger. Feelings are a key part of life that we cannot avoid and should know about.

But how do they fit into our lives as Catholics? Once we understand how feelings fit into the order of our lives, then a lot of the Faith of the Apostles, especially the moral truths, will make more sense. More importantly, we may be able to live our Faith more effectively in true charity.

Jesus Wept, James Tissot

Are Feelings Good or Bad?

The first thing that should be noted is that our passions are a gift from God and of themselves they are good. It is also important to note that the presence of feelings, even the negative ones, are not good or bad. They simply are. The moral quality of our passions occurs by what we decide to do with our feelings. For example, anger is the correct reaction to an unjust situation. If the feeling of anger at injustice helps us to work to rectify the unjust situation, it is good. If it is something that we nourish and then begin to think of ways to harm that person unjustly, then it can become the vice of anger.

The second thing that should be noted is that our passions have been harmed by the Fall, by Original Sin and by our personal sin. In our present fallen state, they don't function like God intended. They are disordered and are disinclined to follow right reason. Sometimes feelings can run amuck or they can lead us toward that which is evil. When feelings are intense, we can't think very well. Sometimes we feel good when we do something bad and feel bad when we do something good. Because of the Fall there are such maladies as mental illness like depression, addiction and schizophrenia. The good news is that Jesus has redeemed our entire nature, including our emotional life. In Him our passions can be healed and restored to their proper place.

How Do Feelings Fit into Our Moral Lives?

Feelings should come third in our moral lives. Using the classical way of speaking, you begin with the intellect, or your mind, to know what is true and good. You should then use your will to act on what you know is right. Assuming you have a well-formed conscience, your passions or feelings can serve as confirmation and accompaniment of what you've done and how good it is. Your feelings must be "governed by reason." In other words, feelings are good companions but lousy guides. To put this process in common language, you have to find out what's right and think about it first, then, you have to believe it, decide it and do it! The resulting or concurrent "feelings" you experience will tell you about what you've done: guilt for bad actions, contented feelings for good actions. This process is called informing your conscience.

Feelings and Conscience

This formation has to be more than just a momentary passing thought right before making a moral decision. It involves a daily, habitual, virtuous formation of your conscience, based on what is true. Once your conscience and moral life are well-tuned, then your feelings will become more ordered and can accurately confirm for you what is right. But when your conscience is not well-formed, your feelings can become inaccurate; you cannot just rely on how you feel to tell good from evil. You have to keep informing your conscience all the time in order for your emotional life to be balanced and accurate. As the *Catechism* says, "Emotions and feelings can be taken up in the virtues or perverted by the vices." It's important to note that in themselves, feelings are neither good nor bad. It is when you choose to *hold on* to a feeling, *that* it can become a vice or a virtue. For example, if someone trips you, it's not sinful to react with feelings of suspicion or anger. But if you decide to hang on to anger and repeat it in a grudge, then it becomes the Capital Sin of Wrath. If you let go of that anger and respond with understanding and forgiveness, that feeling can help you cultivate the theological virtue of love.

This world encourages us to act on feelings first without thinking or commitment, without the use of intellect and will. This results in "enslavement to one's passions." Doing whatever you desire to do is not freedom; it is slavery to those desires! God knows the world of our emotions can be pretty confusing. Jeremiah describes the human heart as "tortuous." St. Paul complains how, "I do not do the good I want, but I do the evil I do not want." Our Lord paints a picture of what it feels like when our emotions are out of control when the house built on sand is buffeted and destroyed in his Parable of the Two Builders.

Indeed, informing your conscience takes more than just intellect and will. Your mind can become darkened and your will can be weakened because of Original Sin and "the world, the flesh and the devil." Feelings can run rampant. We need the outside help of grace, too. This grace is available to us because of what Jesus Christ did for us in his saving Work. It is available in a special way through the Sacraments, prayer, virtuous living and good works, what is called "the ordinary means of sanctification."

Conversation Questions

1. What is another word for "passions"?

2. Are feelings good or bad? Give an example to explain your answer.

3. How do feelings fit into our moral lives?

4. Why do you think that suggestions like "Go with your heart" and "If it feels good, do it" are so popular?

What Our Lord Saw from the Cross

Directions: After viewing and reflecting on the painting, answer the questions below.

James Tissot, What Our Lord Saw from the Cross, 1886–1894.

> ‣ Whom do you see in this painting?

> ‣ From whose point of view are we seeing this scene? How do you know?

> ‣ What experience do you think the artist was trying to give his viewer with this painting?

Catholic Wisdom on Feelings

■ ■

Note: The strips on this Handout are arranged from the simplest statements to the most complex; use the strips that are most appropriate for the students' reading level and maturity. You could also give different strips to different students to provide differentiation.

The passions are natural components of the human psyche [mind].
(CCC 1764)

There are many passions. The most fundamental passion is love.
(CCC 1765)

The principal passions are love and hatred, desire and fear,
joy, sadness, and anger. (CCC 1772)

In themselves passions are neither good nor evil. (CCC 1767)

Emotions and feelings can be taken up in the virtues
or perverted [changed from their original course] by the vices.
(CCC 1774)

To love is to will the good of another. – St. Thomas Aquinas

James 1:6: For the one who doubts is like a wave of the sea
that is driven and tossed about by the wind.

John 16:33: I have told you this so that you might have peace in
me. In the world you will have trouble, but take courage, I have
conquered the world.

By his emotions man intuits the good and suspects evil. (CCC 1771)

Psalm 84:2: My heart and my flesh cry out for the living God.

The proof of love is in the works. Where love exists, it works
great things. But when it ceases to act, it ceases to exist.
– Pope St. Gregory the Great

Thou hast made us for Thyself, O Lord, and our heart is restless
until it finds its rest in Thee. – St. Augustine

When you feel the assaults of passion and anger, then is the time to be silent as Jesus was silent in the midst of ... sufferings. – St. Paul of the Cross

Matthew 7:25-27: The rain fell, the floods came, and the winds blew and buffeted the house. But it did not collapse; it had been set solidly on rock. And everyone who listens to these words of mine but does not act on them will be like a fool who built his house on sand. The rain fell, the floods came, and the winds blew and buffeted the house. And it collapsed and was completely ruined.

The mind commands the body and is instantly obeyed. The mind commands itself and meets resistance. – St. Augustine

It belongs to the perfection of the moral or human good that the passions be *governed by reason*. (CCC 1860)

Romans 13:14: But put on the Lord Jesus Christ, and make no provision for the desires of the flesh.

Jeremiah 17:9-10: More tortuous than anything is the human heart, beyond remedy; who can understand it? I, the LORD, explore the mind and test the heart, giving to all according to their ways, according to the fruit of their deeds.

Mark 7:21-23: From within people, from their hearts, come evil thoughts, unchastity, theft, murder, adultery, greed, malice, deceit, licentiousness, envy, blasphemy, arrogance, folly. All these evils come from within and they defile."

The punishment of every disordered mind is its own disorder. – St. Augustine

Moral perfection consists in man's being moved to the good not by his will alone, but also by his sensitive appetite, as in the words of the psalm: "My heart and flesh sing for joy to the living God. (CCC 1770)

Ignorance of Christ and his Gospel, bad example given by others, enslavement to one's passions, assertion of a mistaken notion of autonomy of conscience, rejection of the Church's authority and her teaching, lack of conversion and of charity: these can be at the source of errors of judgment in moral conduct. (CCC 1792)

Feelings Scenarios

Directions: Read each scenario and answer the questions that follow.

Scenario 1

Juanita was a student in a big school with more than 500 students. It was easy to get lost in the crowd. But Juanita had gone to that school since kindergarten and she had lots of friends. One day a new student named Jane came to the school. While Juanita always had lots of friends to eat lunch with, Jane came into the cafeteria alone and was sitting by herself looking down at the table. Juanita knew she should be more welcoming. She felt sad that Jane was probably lonely. Juanita walked over and invited Jane to sit with her. Jane smiled, and they walked back to the table together. Juanita was pleased to see how much happier Jane seemed now that she was getting a chance to meet some new friends.

1. What feelings does Juanita have in this story?
2. Does Juanita have a well-formed conscience?
3. How do her feelings help her tell right from wrong?

Scenario 2

Bob grew up in a small town and knew everyone there really well. His family often had friends and neighbors over for meals. One day Bob saw on the news that a big group of refugees—people fleeing from bad governments and persecution in other countries—had come to his state. Very few people were helping, and the refugees were homeless and hungry. Bob saw these news stories and knew that wealthier people had a responsibility to help. He felt sad about the hardships the refugees were enduring. He decided to try to convince his family and friends to offer shelter to a refugee family. He felt happy when his parents and two of his neighbors offered to help.

1. What feelings does Bob have in this story?
2. Does Bob have a well-formed conscience?
3. How do his feelings help him tell right from wrong?

Scenario 3

Raymond was a prisoner at a Nazi concentration camp during World War II. A Franciscan friar and priest, he constantly faced harassment and beatings. The guards wanted all the prisoners to live in constant fear, but Raymond countered that fear with love. He shared words of encouragement and even his food with other prisoners. One day the guards were irate because several prisoners had escaped. As punishment, they announced that ten prisoners would be starved to death. One of the condemned men cried out, "Oh, my poor wife, my poor children. I shall never see them again!" When Raymond saw this, he volunteered to take that man's place. Raymond was put in a jail cell. He smiled peacefully at the guards every day until he died.

1. What feelings do you think Raymond had in this story?
2. Does Raymond appear to have a well-formed conscience?
3. How do you think his feelings helped him tell right from wrong?

Scenario 4

It was the 1950s, and Hazel was a high school student in Arkansas. Only white students attended her school. Black students had to go to a separate one across town. When the Supreme Court held that racial segregation in public schools was unconstitutional, her school was forced to integrate. Hazel was not happy about this new rule. She wanted the schools to remain segregated. When the first nine African American students arrived at the high school, a big, angry mob formed. Hazel felt angry too, and she joined the mob. She started walking alongside one of the new students. She expressed her outrage by shouting mean words.

1. What feelings do you think Hazel had in this story?
2. Does Hazel appear to have a well-formed conscience?
3. Should Hazel have followed her heart and gone with her feelings?
4. How should Hazel have behaved differently?

Scenario 5

Andrew was a senior in college. He was a pre-med major, and had already been accepted to several good medical schools. He was happy that his career seemed to be on a firm foundation. Andrew had a girlfriend, Melissa. Melissa was also pre-med, and they planned to marry once they both finished medical school. Melissa became pregnant the summer after college. Andrew and Melissa were both scared, and neither felt ready to be a parent. They decided Melissa would have an abortion so that they could continue with their plans. The night before her appointment, Andrew started to feel very sad and guilty. As a pre-med student, he knew abortion ended a human life. And as a Christian, he knew it was wrong. He went to Melissa's house the next morning and told her he loved her. He told her their plans must change and they must not go through with the abortion. Melissa seemed relieved and happy.

1. What feelings did Andrew have in this story?

2. Does Andrew appear to have a well-formed conscience?

3. How do you think his feelings helped him tell right from wrong?

Answer Key

Sacred Art and the Beatitudes: The Passions in the Christian Life

1. Accept reasoned answers.

2. The figures do not look realistic. Students may say they look dream-like, bright, scary, exaggerated, ominous, intense, desperate. Perhaps the artist used the swirling and rising shapes, distorted perspectives, and so forth, to represent the emotional turmoil of the scene.

3. Jesus, an angel, three men sleeping in the foreground, figures in the background approaching, tree branches, clouds. This painting depicts the Agony in the Garden.

4. Accept reasoned answers.

5. Jesus said, "My soul sorrowful even to death" (Matthew 26:38). He knew the suffering that lay ahead of Him. Accept reasoned answers along these lines.

6. They felt grief (Luke 22:49).

7. Feelings can take control of us if we allow them to. The disciples are so sorrowful that they cannot even stay awake for Jesus when He asked them to. Their feelings have been damaged by Original Sin. Jesus is obedient to the will of the Father despite his feelings. His agony was so intense that He sweat blood. Yet He tells the Father he will go through with His mission. His response to the disciples when they cannot do something as simple as stay awake for Him is appropriate. Jesus doesn't let His feelings overtake Him.

Background Essay

1. Feelings

2. Our passions are a gift from God, and of themselves they are good. The moral quality of our passions occurs by what we decide to do with our feelings. The feeling of anger can be good if it helps you work for justice. The feeling of anger can be bad if you refuse to let go of it and hold a grudge.

3. Feelings should come third, after our intellects and wills.

4. Accept reasoned answers.

The Reality of Sin and Necessity of Virtue

Overview

In a homily he gave just before he became Pope, the then Cardinal Ratzinger stated that we live in a "dictatorship of relativism." Our culture tells us that right and wrong are determined by each individual person and what is right for you may not be right for someone else. However, the Gospel reveals to us that there is right and wrong. The wrong is called sin. All sin is a deprivation of what is true, good, and beautiful. What is right is cultivated and acquired through virtue. In this lesson students will come to understand the reality of sin and the necessity of cultivating virtue in order to overcome it.

Grade Level

 HS

Time

One ninety-minute class

Connection to the Catechism

> CCC 397

> CCC 1846-1864

> CCC 1803-1832

Essential Questions

> Can we truly determine what is good and what is evil?

> Is there really such a thing as an evil or sinful action?

> If sin is real it seems pretty difficult to overcome. How can we truly ever overcome sin?

> Rules limit "freedom," don't they? How can following God's rules set me free?

BIBLICAL TOUCHSTONES

If you act rightly, you will be accepted; but if not, sin lies in wait at the door: its urge is for you, yet you can rule over it.

GENESIS 4:4-7

If anyone sees his brother sinning, if the sin is not deadly, he should pray to God and he will give him life. This is only for those whose sin is not deadly. There is such a thing as deadly sin, about which I do not say that you should pray. All wrongdoing is sin, but there is sin that is not deadly.

1 JOHN 5:16-17

Pietà
BY MICHELANGELO BUONARROTI (C. 1498)

Michelangelo Buonarroti, *Pietà*. Circa 1498. St. Peter's Basilica, Vatican City.

Sacred Art and the Beatitudes
The Reality of Sin and Necessity of Virtue

Pietà, by Michelangelo Buonarroti (c. 1498)

Directions: Take some time to quietly view and reflect on the art. Let yourself be inspired in any way that happens naturally. Then think about the questions below, and discuss them with your classmates.

Conversation Questions

1. What kind of work of art is this? Does the medium (the kind of material the artist used) affect how the art makes you feel?

2. Who are the figures in this painting?

3. What moment does this depict?

4. How would you describe the look on our Lady's face in this sculpture? The Blessed Virgin would have been close to 50 years of age at the time of her Son's death. Why do you think Michelangelo sculpted her as a young lady?

5. Read John 19:25-27 and/or any of the Gospel stories of the Passion of Christ. Why do you think Michelangelo chose not to depict any signs of Jesus' suffering?

6. How does this sculpture show the reality of sin? How does it show us the necessity of virtue?

7. In what ways does this sculpture inspire hope?

8. Say the Hail Holy Queen:

    Hail, holy Queen, Mother of mercy, hail, our life, our sweetness, and our hope. To thee do we cry, poor banished children of Eve: to thee do we send up our sighs, mourning, and weeping in this vale of tears. Turn then, most gracious Advocate, thine eyes of mercy toward us, and after this our exile, show unto us the blessed fruit of thy womb, Jesus, O clement, O loving, O sweet Virgin Mary! Amen.

    How does this prayer, together with the sculpture, help communicate the communion between God and man that Jesus Christ makes possible?

Lesson Plan

Materials

- Background Essay: Recognizing Sin and Seeking Virtue
- Handout A: Good vs. Evil
- Handout B: Scriptural Foundations
- Handout C: Understanding Sin, Virtue, and Natural Consequences

Background/Homework

A. Have students complete **Handout A: Good vs. Evil**.

B. Have students read the **Background Essay: Recognizing Sin and Seeking Virtue** and answer the critical thinking questions.

Warm-Up   *20 minutes*

A. Begin by discussing **Handout A**. If your students are older, consider adding characters such as Atticus Finch, Captain Ahab, Macbeth, etc.

B. After discussing, post different images included in this lesson and ask for student reactions. Images can be found in PowerPoint format in the Catholic Curriculum Exchange at **SophiaInstituteforTeachers.org/curriculum**. *Note: These images are meant to be viewed only by older (11th-12th grade), emotionally mature students. Be certain to preview the images first. Consider sending the images home for parents to determine whether their child is emotionally ready to view them.*

C. Assure students that feeling anger and disgust at the images is perfectly understandable. The images represent truly evil actions. Then pose the question: If we can say these things are evil, why then would it not be okay to say other things are immoral? How can it possibly make sense to ever say that something can be "right for you but not for me"? Is it possible to judge actions without judging people's hearts?

Activity

60 minutes

A. Pass out **Handout B: Scriptural Foundations**. Read Genesis chapter 3 aloud while students follow along. Then discuss aloud the questions that follow. Repeat the process with the story of David and Goliath.

B. Emphasize the definitions of sin and virtue found in the *Catechism*.

C. Watch and then discuss the video:

 Lifehouse's Everything Skit
Found at: http://youtu.be/cyheJ48OLYA

D. Have students complete **Handout C: Understanding Sin, Virtue, and Natural Consequences**. Reconvene as a large group to share ideas.

Wrap-Up

10 minutes

As a class, decide the one or two vices to avoid and virtues to cultivate as a group for the remainder of the year. Come up with practical things you can do to work on both of these goals, and post a list in your classroom throughout the year.

Extension Options

A. Have students write a short story or put together a skit that clearly shows the struggle between good and evil. They should have characters that clearly exemplify both. Within the story it should be clear that the hero of the story had to possess and cultivate virtue in order to overcome the villain. Students should include a 1-2 page explanation of the symbolism found within their story and how it communicates the reality of sin and necessity of virtue through the plot and characters.

B. Have students compare and contrast the two paintings on **Handout B**.

Recognizing Sin and Seeking Virtue

Elisabeth could hardly eat breakfast she was so filled with nervous excitement! Elisabeth was a great softball player. She and her best friend Jane had played on the same county teams for years, and they had both made it onto their highly selective high school team. Last week their coach announced that a scout was coming from a nearby college to look for excellent players. Elisabeth wanted to go to college, and an athletic scholarship would make it more affordable. She had been practicing longer and harder than usual in the days leading up to the visit and finally the day had come. As she was getting her things ready to go, Elisabeth's phone rang. She heard Jane's voice on the line: "I have bad news—the scout had a change of plans and he won't be coming till next week." The game would be postponed till then. Elisabeth was disappointed, but at least she would have another week to build up her skills even more!

The next afternoon when she arrived at practice, Elisabeth heard her teammates talking excitedly. They were all crowded around Jane, who was beaming with pride. "What's going on?" she asked her friend.

Jane smiled sheepishly. "The scout came yesterday." she said. Then she burst into a smile. "I played really well, and he said it's almost a sure thing they will offer me a scholarship. Isn't that exciting?"

Elisabeth was confused. "You lied to me?" she asked.

Return of the Prodigal Son, Bartolome Esteban Murillo

"I would never have gotten noticed by that scout if you were there because you play so much better than I do. I had to do something!" Jane tossed her pony tail.

"So you did lie. And now my chances for a scholarship are gone!" Elizabeth dropped her bag of equipment. She stared at her friend. "How could you do something so wrong?"

Jane shrugged. "What does "wrong" mean anyway? It was right for me at the time. And it worked; it looks like I am getting a scholarship."

In a 2005 homily just before he became pope, the then Cardinal Ratzinger, Benedict XVI, said, "We are building a dictatorship of relativism that does not recognize anything as definitive and whose ultimate goal consists solely of one's own ego and desires." Previously in 2003, he also stated that, "relativism—which considers all opinions as true, even if they are contradictory—is the greatest problem of our time."

What exactly is this philosophy of moral relativism? Do you see relativism in Jane's thinking in the story above? Why does Pope Benedict XVI think it is so damaging? It is damaging because it holds that there is no such thing as right and wrong. If you consider something "right" for you, it is. What is right for one person, it says, might be wrong for someone else, and vice versa. Because moral relativism holds that something is only a sin if one personally believes it is wrong, moral relativism negates the concept of sin entirely. According to moral relativism, the only thing that is always wrong is to be "judgmental."

Right and Wrong Exist

The natural order of the world clearly teaches that there is right and wrong. This is what we call the "natural law." Any human being is able to know this law through the use of reason, regardless of history, culture, or religion. Moreover, the Gospel reveals to us that there is clearly a right way to live and a wrong way to live. In fact, the entire drama of Salvation History shows us that there is a struggle of good vs. evil in people's hearts. In order for us to live the lives God intended for us to live, we must have a clear understanding of what evil and sin are and—more importantly—what the good and virtues are. As human beings created in the image of God, we are naturally drawn to the true, the good, and the beautiful. Very often, evil and sin are distortions of those things. The Devil uses those distortions to try to draw us away from that which is true, good, and beautiful.

The Reality of Sin

So what is evil? What is sin? Evil is the absence of good. God does not create evil. Evil comes about when people use their free will to reject goodness. What then is sin? According to the *Catechism of the Catholic Church*, "Sin is an offense against reason, truth, and right conscience; it is failure in genuine love for God and neighbor caused by a perverse attachment to certain goods. It wounds the nature of man and injures human solidarity. It has been defined as 'an utterance, a deed, or a desire contrary to the eternal law.'" (CCC 1849)

All sin is evil, but not all sins carry the same degree of evil. Here we can distinguish between mortal sin and venial sin. "*Mortal sin* destroys charity in the heart of man by a grave violation of God's law; it turns man away from God, who is his ultimate end and his beatitude, by preferring an inferior good to him. *Venial sin* allows charity to subsist, even though it offends and wounds it" (CCC 1855). In other words, mortal sin is a grave and serious sin in which we choose to sever our relationship with God. Venial sin is less serious and, while it hurts our relationship with God, it does not sever it. While venial sin does not sever our relationship with God, it is important to work against it because if we don't, venial sin will lead to

The Seven Virtues, Anton Francesco dello Scheggia

mortal sin. In order for a sin to be mortal it must meet three criteria: 1) grave matter, 2) one has to have full knowledge that it is wrong, and 3) one has to give complete consent and do it anyway.

As Christians we are called to recognize first and foremost that sin exists in our own lives, to repent, and to entrust ourselves to the mercy of God. We must also recognize that sin exists in the world and that others are capable of sin as well. Love means desiring what is best for a person. To declare with charity that something sinful is sinful is not to be judgmental. It is to speak the truth with love, because you desire what is best for someone: eternal beatitude.

The Necessity of Virtue

The good news of this truth, however, is that there is redemption. There is grace, and there is mercy. God desires to forgive us of our sins. There are also ways we can grow and overcome sin. Virtue is necessary to overcome sin. We are called to cultivate virtue in our lives. To live a virtuous life is to live the good life, and to experience truth, beauty, and goodness in all its fullness.

What Is a Virtue?

The word virtue comes from the Latin "vir" meaning man, manliness or power. Virtue is "a habitual and firm disposition to do the good" (CCC 1803). In simple terms, to build virtue is to build good habits, so that doing good becomes natural and brings you joy. When we sin we build bad habits and vices. When we make virtuous decisions, we build good habits that turn into virtues. This takes time and effort, but it is worth it: As we attain and grow in virtue in our lives, we come to experience true joy and happiness because virtue brings us closer to God. When we exercise our freedom for the sake of loving God and one another we become like God.

Like with any discipline, cultivating virtue is hard at first. But it eventually becomes easier and even pleasurable. Think about how it works to learn any new skill. It's hard at first, but then gets easier and more fun as you get better at it. A first-time runner feels burdened by the need to train and can barely run around the block without getting winded. But with discipline, she begins to look forward to running every day and eventually can enter a marathon. A new piano student dreads playing scales over and over. But with discipline, he can start playing more challenging and beautiful pieces. It's always more fun to do something when you're good at it. You become good at things through discipline. And just like sports, or playing an instrument, cultivating virtue leads to happiness. But more than that, cooperating with God's grace through virtue is the only way to find true happiness. Without virtue we cannot overcome sin.

The virtues are divided into two major categories: The Cardinal, or natural virtues, and the theological virtues. The Cardinal or natural virtues are Temperance, Prudence, Justice and Fortitude. These are essentially the four pillars on which all the other virtues rest.

Grace builds upon nature with the theological virtues, which are: faith, hope, and charity. These are the virtues we receive in seed form at our baptism. It is then up to

us through cooperation in the life of Christ to cultivate and allow those virtues to come to fruition in our lives. For this reason virtue is both the seed and the fruit of a deep and personal relationship with Christ. It is what allows us to be receptive to grace, as well what comes out of that cooperation.

In today's culture it can be very difficult to declare these truths of sin and virtue. Many people today do not even believe that there is such a thing as good and evil, or of virtue and sin. Instead of virtues – habits like courage, temperance, etc., that are always good, regardless of circumstance – we talk about "values," a word which implies the definition of good and evil are relative (or, in other words, nonexistent).

When we eliminate virtue, we eliminate the chance to build a society that truly desires the good of others and seeks truth. We must seek truth, beauty and goodness. If we seek virtue we will find truth, beauty, and goodness. If we seek virtue we are given the weapons to fight sin and evil.

Conversation Questions

1. How does the example of Jane's behavior show that a wrong action can never be "right for me"?
2. What is moral relativism?
3. Can two contradictory things be true? Explain.
4. Does God create evil?
5. How does cultivating virtue help us resist sin?

Good vs. Evil

■

Directions: Below is a list of characters from literature and film. On the line next to each name, write whether the character is good or evil. If you are uncertain, you may do a little research about the movie or story to try and figure it out.

Good or Evil?

_____   1. Luke Skywalker (*Star Wars* Trilogy)

_____   2. Lord Voldemort (*Harry Potter*)

_____   3. Frodo Baggins (*Lord of the Rings*)

_____   4. President Snow (*The Hunger Games*)

_____   5. Harry Potter (*Harry Potter*)

_____   6. Darth Vader (*Star Wars* Trilogy)

_____   7. Sauron (*Lord of the Rings*)

_____   8. Rapunzel (*Tangled*)

_____   9. Katniss Everdeen (*The Hunger Games*)

_____   10. Mother Gothel (*Tangled*)

_____   11. Peter Parker (*Spiderman*)

_____   12. Cruella De Vil (*101 Dalmatians*)

_____   13. Aslan (*Narnia* Series)

_____   14. Bruce Wayne (*Batman*)

_____   15. The White Witch (*The Lion, the Witch and the Wardrobe*)

_____   16. Ursula (*The Little Mermaid*)

17. Come up with your own example of one good and one evil character from your favorite film or book and write each in the space provided.

   › Good _____

   › Evil _____

18. Why did you write "evil" for the characters you did? What do they all have in common? What made each of them evil?

19. Why did you write "good" for the characters that you did? What do they all have in common?

20. What are the basic differences between good and evil?

Scriptural Foundations

Directions: Read the following Scripture passages and answer the questions that follow.

Genesis 3

Expulsion from Eden

1. What was the sin of Adam and Eve?
2. What are the consequences of this sin?
3. What role does the serpent play in this sin?
4. How does God continue to show His love for Adam and Eve even though He punishes them for their sin?
5. In what ways does this sin affect the rest of their (and our) story?

1 Samuel 17

David and Goliath

6. Based on this story, what qualities does David possess?
7. What is another name for these qualities?
8. Would David have been able to defeat Goliath without these qualities? Why or why not?
9. What connections from this story can we make to our own lives and the reality of the Christian life?
10. What is the definition of sin? What is the definition of virtue?

Understanding Sin, Virtue, and Natural Consequences

Directions: Complete the chart below. In the first column give an example of a sin. In the second column give examples of possible consequences for that sin. In the third column list any virtues that would be helpful in overcoming the sin. Finally, give examples of possible positive consequences for living out those virtues in the fourth column. Refer to *Catechism* paragraphs 1803-1832 and 1846-1864 for assistance. An example has been done for you.

Sin	Possible Consequences	Virtue(s) Needed	Positive Consequences
Stealing	Jail time, fines, causing harm to others, living in fear of getting caught	Charity, temperance, patience, honesty	Learning the value of hard work to acquire something, respect, enjoyment of goods.

Answer Key

Sacred Art and the Beatitudes:
The Reality of Sin and the Necessity of Virtue

1. Sculpture. Accept reasoned answers.

2. Jesus Christ and the Virgin Mary

3. A moment after the Death of Jesus on the Cross.

4. She looks sad but peaceful. She accepts the reality of her Son's death. Accept reasoned answers.

5. Accept reasoned answers.

6. The sculpture confronts us with the reality of sin by showing us our deceased Lord, who died for our sins. He is held by His mother, the immaculate Virgin Mary. Mary was the embodiment of virtue. Both Jesus and Mary help us see how cultivating virtue can help us avoid sin and face suffering while remaining obedient to God.

7. Accept reasoned answers.

8. Although the moment the sculpture shows was one of great suffering, both Jesus and Mary look serene. Jesus has conquered sin and death. Sanctification through Christ makes communion between God and man possible.

Background Essay

1. Deception for personal gain is wrong; for Jane to trick her friend was wrong. For Jane to steal Elizabeth's chances at a scholarship was wrong. The actions are always wrong, no matter who is judging them.

2. Moral relativism is the outlook that all opinions are equally valid.

3. No.

4. No. Evil is the absence of good. Humans can choose to behave in evil ways through our own free will.

5. Cultivating virtue helps us do good. Doing good helps dispose us to grace, so we may better cooperate with the Lord and do His will. When we are virtuous, doing good becomes something that makes us happy, and we want to do good even more.

Handout A

1. Good
2. Evil
3. Good
4. Evil
5. Good
6. Evil
7. Evil
8. Good
9. Good
10. Evil
11. Good
12. Evil
13. Good
14. Good
15. Evil
16. Evil
17. Accept reasoned answers

18. They caused harm to others, they desired destruction. They put their own comfort and pleasure over the good of others. They wanted bad things to happen to others in order for themselves to succeed. Accept additional reasoned answers.

19. They desired to do good and/or put a stop to those who were oppressing others. They desired what was best for their world. They showed virtue. They put the good of others over their own comfort or pleasure. Accept additional reasoned answers.

20. Good seeks what is best for others while evil seeks its own interests and destroys the happiness of others. Good is loving. Evil is unloving and selfish. Accept additional reasoned answers.

Handout B

1. Disobedience. Failing to trust in God. Ultimately it was a sin of pride. Accept additional reasoned answers.

2. Woman: "I will intensify your toil in childbearing; in pain you shall bring forth children. Yet your urge shall be for your husband, and he shall rule over you." (Pain during childbirth, strife in the relationship with her husband, the woman will struggle to understand her role as a woman.)

   Man: "Cursed is the ground because of you! In toil you shall eat its yield all the days of your life. Thorns and thistles it shall bear for you, and you shall eat the grass of the field. By the sweat of your brow you shall eat bread." (Work and labor become difficult, the relationships between him and the earth and between him and his wife are damaged.)

   Both: Death, banishment from the garden and God's presence.

3. The serpent provided the temptation. "Man, tempted by the devil, let his trust in his Creator die in his heart and, abusing his freedom, disobeyed God's command" (CCC 397). The devil wants us to sin so we can be separated from God just as he is. Every

action against God is a reflection of the devil's desires rather than God's. Accept additional reasoned answers.

4. Even though He is banishing them from the Garden, He still takes the time to clothe them. He tells the snake that there will be a battle between the snake's offspring and Eve's offspring, and that Eve's will win (Genesis 3:15). Theologians call this announcement the protoevangelium, or first Gospel (CCC 410).

5. Immediately following this event we have the first murder in the story of Cain and Abel. Then follows the Flood. Noah and his sons sin. We then see that in the remainder of the Old Testament God's people struggle between sin and doing the right thing. There is disorder in the human race and humanity struggles constantly to find happiness and live in a way that brings them true joy. Accept additional reasoned answers.

6. He exhibits bravery, courage, fortitude, trust in God, piety, humility, concern for others, prudence. Accept additional reasoned answers.

7. Virtues

8. No, because without them he would either not have accepted the challenge to fight Goliath and if he had gone in foolishly he would have been defeated. Accept additional reasoned answers.

9. In many ways Goliath represents sin in our lives. We can often feel as if sin is so big that we are powerless against it. There are sin and obstacles in our lives. If we face them alone, without God's grace and without cultivating virtue, sin will defeat us. However, if we throw ourselves into the arms of Christ, trust in His mercy and strength, and work to grow in virtue, then God will give us the grace to overcome the "giants" in our own life. Accept additional reasoned answers.

10. Sin is an offense against reason, truth, and right conscience; it is failure in genuine love for God and neighbor caused by a perverse attachment to certain goods. It wounds the nature of man and injures human solidarity. It has been defined as "an utterance, a deed, or a desire contrary to the eternal law" (CCC 1849). Virtue is the habit of doing good. A virtuous person tends toward the good with all his sensory and spiritual powers; he pursues the good and chooses it in concrete actions (CCC 1803).

Handout C

Below is an example. Accept additional reasoned answers.

Sin	Possible Consequences	Virtue(s) Needed	Positive Consequences
Fornication	Sexually transmitted diseases, out-of-wedlock pregnancy, difficulty in marriage, depression, selfishness	Purity, chastity, fortitude, charity	True appreciation for the opposite sex, greater chance at lasting marriage, unselfishness
Drunkenness	Making bad decisions you wouldn't normally make when sober, driving drunk and injuring or killing someone, losing control, alcoholism	Temperance, fortitude	More authentic relationships, happier times, appreciating activities and goods in moderation, making controlled decisions
Lying	Loss of trust, making others feel foolish, feeling embarrassed at being caught in a lie, guilt for deceiving friends.	Honesty, courage	Regaining the trust of loved ones and friends, feeling encouraged, being freed from a web of deception

Teacher Notes

Obedience

Overview

Doing God's will by obeying His commandments is the only way to find happiness. With God's grace and the help of the Holy Spirit, we can strive to listen to and obey God's will. Throughout salvation history, God has revealed His love for humans and His desire for each person to be happy with Him in heaven forever. To live a life of true happiness, each person must strive to hear God's will and live it every day. Humanity from Adam and Eve to the present time has struggled to do God's will and all too often has fallen into sin by pride and selfishness.

Grade Levels

 ES ■ MS ■ HS

Time

Two fifty-minute classes

Connection to the Catechism

› CCC 144

› CCC 146

› CCC 148

Essential Questions

› If I have to obey rules, doesn't that mean I am not free?

› Where can I find God's plan for happiness?

› How have others found joy in following God's will or unhappiness in disobeying Him?

BIBLICAL TOUCHSTONES

I will bless you and make your descendants as countless as the stars of the sky and the sands of the seashore; your descendants will take possession of the gates of their enemies, and in your descendants all the nations of the earth will find blessing, because you obeyed my command.

GENESIS 22:17-18

As the Father loves me, so I also love you. Remain in my love. If you keep my commandments, you will remain in my love, just as I have kept my Father's commandments and remain in his love.

JOHN 15:10

The Annunciation

BY LEONARDO DA VINCI (C. 1472)

Leonardo da Vinci, The Annunciation.
c. 1472. Oil on Panel, Uffizi Gallery, Florence, Italy.

Sacred Art and the Beatitudes
Obedience

 The Annunciation, by Leonardo da Vinci (c. 1472)

Directions: Take some time to quietly view and reflect on the art. Let yourself be inspired in any way that happens naturally. Then think about the questions below, and discuss them with your classmates.

Conversation Questions

1. When you first look at this painting, what do you notice? What is your favorite part of the painting and why?

2. Who are the figures in this painting?

3. What is this event known as?

4. What do you notice about the overall composition of the painting: the colors, the background, the lighting, etc.?

5. Read Luke 1:26-30. What does the archangel Gabriel tell the Blessed Virgin Mary? How does she feel at first? What is her response to the news she receives?

6. The Blessed Virgin Mary is a perfect example of obedience. Why?

7. What would your reaction be if an angel told you about a special mission God wanted you to carry out?

Lesson Plan

Materials

- › Holy Bible
- › Handout A: Why Should I Obey?
- › Handout B: Is Obedience Justified?
- › Handout C: Example of Disobedience in Sacred Scripture
- › Handout D: Example of Obedience in Sacred Scripture
- › Handout E: Example of Disobedience in Sacred Scripture
- › Handout F: Example of Obedience in Sacred Scripture
- › Handout G: Sharing My Family's Example of How Obedience Can Work

Background/Homework   *15 minutes the day before*

For homework, have students discuss with a family member such as a parent, grandparent, or sibling how obedience has helped him or her live a better life. (Students should tell the family member that this witness will be shared in class.)

Warm-Up   *20 minutes*

A. Ask students to imagine themselves in the future, as parents of a young child. (Alternatively, you may ask them to imagine they have suddenly received a new kitten or puppy to take care of.) Working independently, have them jot down 3 or 4 simple rules they would make for their child/pet.

B. Walk around the room as students work, and write some examples from student work on the board, for example:

- › Eat nutritious food
- › Exercise regularly
- › Don't cross the street by yourself
- › Don't touch the stove

C. After a few minutes, ask students:

- › Did most of you write rules similar to the ones on the board?
- › Why did you choose these types of rules? (Students will likely say that the rules were for the child's/pet's own protection, or for their own good.)
- › If you love someone, don't you want what's best for them?

> Would any loving parent have **no rules** for their young child? Of course not. Why not?

D. Note: With the youngest students, you may wish to use **Handout A: Why Should I Obey?**

Lead students to the conclusion that if you love someone, you want him or her to be safe and happy. This is how God feels about us. Sin hurts us and makes us sad. When He created us, he told us what we need to do in order to be happy and avoid wounding ourselves. But, as far back as Adam and Eve, we have had trouble obeying. We often feel that rules tie us down. But the truth is, God's rules free us — they free us to choose good and avoid evil, so we can be truly happy.

E. Ask students if obedience means blindly following orders, no matter what they are. Project a copy of **Handout B: Is Obedience Justified?** Reveal one statement at a time, and then discuss the critical thinking questions.

Lead students to the conclusion that obedience is required when someone is in a position of just authority over you (a parent, a teacher, a duly elected official, etc.) and when a command itself is moral, that is, it does not conflict with the Ten Commandments or fail to show love to God and one's neighbor. Those in just authority should be obeyed even if their reasons for certain rules are not clear. But when you know someone loves you and wants the best for you, obedience comes much more easily.

Activity

30 minutes

A. Students will now go on a scavenger hunt through Scripture for obedience and disobedience. First, ask students to recall examples of obedience and disobedience they already know. For example:

› Adam and Eve disobey God and eat from the tree of knowledge of good and evil.

› Cain murders his brother.

› Noah obeys God and builds an ark.

› Lot's wife disobeys the angel's instructions not to look back at Sodom.

› Abraham obeys God's commands to leave his homeland, and to sacrifice his son.

› The Blessed Virgin obeys God's will in becoming the mother of Jesus.

› Jesus always obeys the will of the Father.

B. Preview the provided Scripture passages on **Handouts C–F** and determine which ones are the best fit for your students' reading level. Use those, and feel free to make any extras with favorite or recently covered Bible stories.

C. Make enough copies of **Handouts C–G** to give one to every student in the class. Split up students into five groups. Arrange desks to make a common table per group. On the first table, place a stack of copies of **Handout C**. On the second table, place a stack of copies of **Handout D**. Continue on all tables all handouts through **Handout G**. Have students take a copy of the Handout at their table and complete as directed.

D. After a few minutes, have each group rotate to another station, taking their Handouts with them. Repeat until each group has completed all Handouts.

Wrap-Up

A. Read aloud to the class from Luke 22:39-46, the Agony in the Garden. On the board, write the scripture verse.

For just as through the disobedience of the one person the many were made sinners, so through the obedience of one the many will be made righteous (Romans 5:19).

B. As a large group, discuss how Jesus demonstrates the virtue of obedience. Then have students compare and contrast, as St. Paul does, what happens in the Garden of Gethsemane with the Garden of Eden.

Extension Options

A. Have students skim over their activity sheets and circle a few key words that express truth about happiness and obedience. Then, as a group, have them list the words in a Wordle, a Power Point, or poster. Have each group discuss their insights, and write a prayer expressing their desire to experience happiness through obedience.

B. For homework, have students read the story of the rich young man in Matthew 19 together with their parents. How does this story help us understand obedience? Is happiness found in material comforts, or in a higher purpose?

Following God's Will through Obedience ■ ■

The word "obedience" doesn't sound like fun. In fact, our culture tends to view the idea of obedience negatively. We often think it is children, not freethinking adults, who should obey. Adults who have to obey are oppressed! Modern Disney princesses even sing about how great it supposedly is to not to have to obey: "No right, no wrong, no rules for me: I'm free!" belts out Queen Elsa.

No rules might sound like fun at first. But would lack of rules truly be a good thing?

Obedience and Happiness

Obeying good rules results in greater happiness. What if drivers refused to obey rules of the road? What if athletes refused to obey their coach? Or a surgical student refused to obey his medical school professor? Great harm would result, and no one would be better off. In each case, the rules enforced are designed to promote such virtues as safety, goodness, harmony, fairness, courage, selflessness, patience, hard work, and personal growth. Since the beginning of time, just rules and obedience to them has resulted in human flourishing. Those in authority reflect the beneficence of God and carry a responsibility to guide others to goodness and virtue. It makes it easier to obey parents, coaches, or teachers, and others when we know they want what is best for us, just like God does. But when those in authority act out of selfishness, harm can result.

Agony in the Garden, Pietro Perugino

The individual's well-formed conscience is key to Catholic teaching on obedience, and there is no obligation to obey unjust rules or commands. Unfortunately, history is full of examples of bad governments that have demanded obedience when it was not justified. Hitler's Germany, Stalin's Russia, and Pol Pot's Cambodia are just a few tragic examples. Obedience does not mean blindly carrying out whatever orders one is given. "Authority is exercised legitimately only when it seeks the common good of the group concerned and if it employs morally licit means to attain it. If rulers were to enact unjust laws or take measures contrary to the moral order, such arrangements would not be binding in conscience" (CCC 1903).

Obedience in Scripture

Sacred Scripture offers many examples of how obeying results in human flourishing and how disobedience damages the transgressor and others. In preparing to consider examples in Scripture as well as real life, consider the beautiful teaching about obedience which the Catholic Church offers:

To obey (from the Latin *ob-audire*, to "hear or listen to") in faith is to submit freely to the word that has been heard, because its truth is guaranteed by God, who is Truth itself. Jesus always obeyed the will of the Father. Other models of obedience include Abraham and the Virgin Mary, who is its most perfect embodiment (CCC 144).

God gave Adam and Eve the gift of life, which was immediately followed by a gift of rules for happiness: He ordered Adam not to eat from the tree of knowledge of good and evil. Freedom for the Israelites was immediately followed by the gift of the Ten Commandments, revealed to Moses on Mount Sinai. The precious gift of life in Jesus Christ comes with the Great Commandment and the teachings of the Sermon on the Mount. These rules are not to inhibit our freedom; they are to help us achieve it in this life and the next. "For freedom Christ set us free" (Galatians 5:1). This is the truth about obedience that modern culture gets wrong. Sin is what has made obedience feel oppressive.

Freedom in Christ

God has revealed Himself and His loving plan for human flourishing in the Deposit of Faith which includes Sacred Tradition and Sacred Scripture. Jesus has promised the Holy Spirit Who acts through His Church to guide all to the best we can be, to our eternal salvation. God has given us the Ten Commandments and the Beatitudes to live a life filled with joy and to impact the lives of others so they can be happy too.

Jesus Himself tells us that He wants us to be happy. In John 15:9-13 He says, "As the Father loves me, so I also love you. Remain in my love. If you keep my commandments, you will remain in my love, just as I have kept my Father's commandments and remain in his love." Jesus wants us to experience the kind of awesome love that He enjoys!

There is another reason why He wants us to keep the commandments. He says, "I have told you this so that my joy may be in you and your joy may be complete. This is my commandment: love one another as I love you." If obeying means experiencing love and joy, would you obey?

Jesus gives us the way to incredible happiness. He is the most trusted authority. Since we can't go wrong by following obeying and listening to Jesus, let's help each other and ourselves do just that.

Conversation Questions

1. Does obedience mean doing everything you're told?

2. How does your conscience apply to obedience?

3. Reflect on Galatians 5:1: "For freedom Christ has set us free." Write a summary statement explaining why this statement is true.

Why Should I Obey?

Teacher Note: Project a copy of this handout using an overhead or touchscreen. Reveal one statement/question at a time. After each one, ask the class why such a rule would exist. Lead students to the truth that in each case, parents have put a rule in place so their child will not get hurt. Sin hurts us, and God does not want us, His children, to get hurt.

1. Jane's parents have a wood stove in their living room. It heats their whole house and keeps everyone warm. The wood stove gets very hot and anyone who touches it will get burned. Jane's parents tell her not to touch the stove.

   Why would Jane's parents make this rule? Why should Jane obey?

2. Bob lives on a busy street. Cars and trucks drive by all day and all through the night. Bob's parents tell him not to go out in the front yard by himself, and never to cross the street without them.

   Why would Bob's parents make this rule? Why should Bob obey?

3. Carlos's dad uses a wood saw in their garage. He makes furniture with the saw by cutting wood and shaping it carefully. The saw has a very sharp blade. Carlos's parents tell him never to touch the saw.

   Why would Carlos's parents make this rule? Why should Carlos obey?

4. The Lord tells us not to kill.

   Why did God give us this rule? Why should we obey?

5. The Lord tells us not to steal.

   Why did God give us this rule? Why should we obey?

6. The Lord tells us not to lie.

   Why did God give us this rule? Why should we obey?

7. Why did God give us rules like the Ten Commandments? Why should we obey?

Should You Obey?

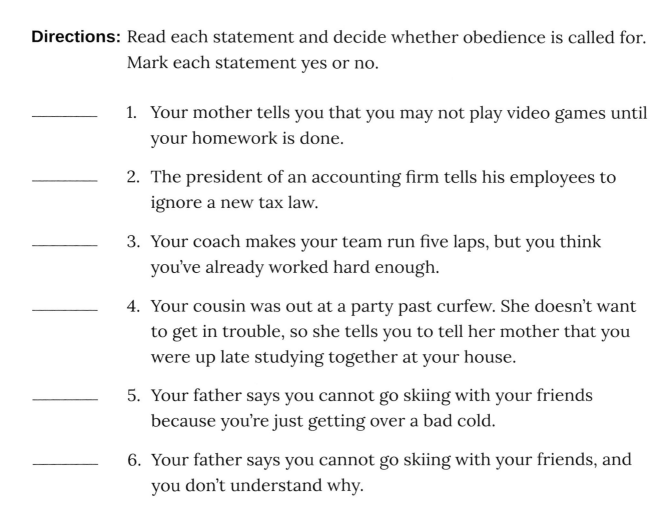

Directions: Read each statement and decide whether obedience is called for. Mark each statement yes or no.

_____ 1. Your mother tells you that you may not play video games until your homework is done.

_____ 2. The president of an accounting firm tells his employees to ignore a new tax law.

_____ 3. Your coach makes your team run five laps, but you think you've already worked hard enough.

_____ 4. Your cousin was out at a party past curfew. She doesn't want to get in trouble, so she tells you to tell her mother that you were up late studying together at your house.

_____ 5. Your father says you cannot go skiing with your friends because you're just getting over a bad cold.

_____ 6. Your father says you cannot go skiing with your friends, and you don't understand why.

Critical Thinking Questions

1. Obedience is required for numbers 1, 3, 5, and 6. On the other hand, it would be wrong to "obey" for numbers 2 and 4. What are some reasons why?

2. It can be harder to obey when you don't understand the reasons for a rule or command. What makes it hard? Does this mean you shouldn't obey? In cases like this, is there anything that can make it easier to obey?

Example of Disobedience in Sacred Scripture

Directions: Read the following Scripture passage and respond to the reflection prompts.

Genesis 3:1-13; 15-19

Reflection Prompts

1. To whom did Eve listen?

2. What did she do?

3. To whom did Adam listen?

4. What did he do?

5. How did disobeying God's will impact the lives of Adam and Eve?

6. What is your reaction to this story? What does this story tell us about obeying God?

After responding to the above questions, discuss your answers as a group. Write at least two ideas from other group members.

1.

2.

Example of Obedience in Sacred Scripture

Directions: Read the following Scripture passage and respond to the reflection prompts.

> **Genesis 12:1-9; 17:1-8**

Reflection Prompts

1. How did Abram obey God?

2. What was the result of Abram's listening to God and doing His will?

3. What is your reaction to this story? What does this story tell us about obeying God?

After responding to the above questions, discuss your answers as a group. Write at least two ideas from other group members.

1.

2.

Example of Disobedience in Sacred Scripture

Directions: Read the following Scripture passage and respond to the reflection prompts.

> **2 Samuel 11:1 to 12:18a**

Reflection Prompts

1. When we sin, we often are blind to having done wrong. How does David show spiritual blindness?

2. When we sin, we often are blind to the harm it causes. What harm does David's sins cause?

3. Which of the Ten Commandments does David break?

4. What does this story tell us about the connection between obeying God's commandments and happiness?

After responding to the above questions, discuss your answers as a group. Write at least two ideas from other group members.

1.

2.

Example of Obedience in Sacred Scripture

Directions: Read the following Scripture passage and respond to the reflection prompts.

> **Luke 1:26-38; 46-49**

Reflection Prompts

1. Elaborate upon Mary's reaction to being the mother of Jesus. What else may Mary have been thinking?

2. What would your reaction be if an angel told you about an important mission God wanted you to carry out? Would you follow through?

3. What does this story tell us about obeying God?

After responding to the above questions, discuss your answers as a group. Write at least 2 ideas from other group members.

1.

2.

Sharing My Family's Example of How Obedience Can Work

Directions: In a round-robin fashion, share your family stories in your small group. Write an idea you find important for each group member's story. Use your own paper if needed.

Group member name: _____

Idea about the importance of obedience: _____

_____

_____

Group member name: _____

Idea about the importance of obedience: _____

_____

_____

Group member name: _____

Idea about the importance of obedience: _____

_____

_____

Group member name: _____

Idea about the importance of obedience: _____

_____

_____

Group member name: _____

Idea about the importance of obedience: _____

_____

_____

Answer Key

Sacred Art and the Beatitudes: Obedience

1. Accept reasoned answers.

2. The archangel Gabriel and the Blessed Virgin Mary

3. The Annunciation

4. Accept reasoned answers.

5. Gabriel calls Mary "Full of grace." He tells her that she has found favor with God, and that she will be the mother of the Lord. She is confused at first. She then consents to what the angel tells her.

6. Mary is happy to obey. She says, "Behold, I am the handmaid of the Lord. May it be done to me according to your word" (Luke 1:38). Despite her initial confusion, and despite what an overwhelming piece of news this was for her to receive, she is joyful in her consent.

7. Accept reasoned answers.

Jesus Teaches Us How to Live

Overview

Jesus is the perfect model of human life. Throughout His earthly ministry He realizes each of the Beatitudes providing us with concrete examples of how we must be open to God's saving love and keep His commandments if we want to have eternal life. As Catholics, we are called to be Christ in the world and build His Kingdom through our actions. Works of mercy are concrete ways in which we can live out our faith. In Scripture, Christ not only instructs us on what the acts of mercy are, He also provides examples in His ministry.

Grade Levels

 ES MS

Time

Two fifty-minute classes

Connection to the Catechism

- CCC 1966-1970
- CCC 2447

Essential Questions

- What are the seven Corporal Works of Mercy?
- Why are they important?
- How does Christ model these works?
- How can I perform these works today?

BIBLICAL TOUCHSTONES

The Lord is gracious and merciful, slow to anger and abounding in mercy.

PSALM 145:8

Amen I say to you, whatever you did for one of these least brothers of mine, you did for me.

MATTHEW 25:40

The Transfiguration
BY BL. FRA ANGELICO, GUIDO DI PIETRO (C. 1395–1455)

Bl. Fra Angelico, Guido di Pietro (c. 1395 - February 18, 1455) from
The Transfiguration In Cell 6 of the Convent of San Marco, Museo di San Marco, Florence.

DIGITAL IMAGES AVAILABLE AT
WWW.SOPHIAINSTITUTEFORTEACHERS.ORG

Sacred Art and the Beatitudes
Jesus Teaches Us How to Live

The Transfiguration, by Bl. Fra Angelico (c. 1395–1455)

Directions: Take some time to quietly view and reflect on the art. Let yourself be inspired in any way that happens naturally. Then think about the questions below, and discuss them with your classmates.

Conversation Questions

1. Whom do you see in this fresco? Which luminous mystery of the Rosary is depicted?

2. How do the colors, light, and other aspects of the painting make you feel?

3. What are some words you would use to describe how Jesus looks in this painting? What is He standing on?

4. Read Matthew 17:1-9. How does this painting help you understand these verses?

5. The Blessed Virgin Mary and St. Dominic were not present at the Transfiguration. Why might the artist have included them in this painting?

6. How do the Apostles react to what is happening? What does Jesus say to them in the Bible?

7. How does that same message, "Do not be afraid," come through to everyone who sees this fresco? Why is it such an important message for all Christians?

8. Compare this work to Ford Maddox Brown's painting, "Jesus Washing Peter's Feet." (*Images can be found at SophiaInstituteforTeachers.org/libraryart or on page ix of this guide.*) How do these paintings together show us who Jesus is?

Lesson Plan

Student Materials

- Handout A: Hunter's Story—"Coming Home"
- Note-Taking Aid
- Handout B: Christ Our Teacher (1 of 3)
- Enrichment Essay: Jesus Teaches Us How to Live
- Handout C: Living the Values of the Kingdom of God
- Handout D: Living Like Christ

Background/Homework

Have students read **Handout A: Hunter's Story – "Coming Home"** and answer the questions.

Warm-Up Activity   *10 minutes*

A. Have a student summarize the story from the homework

B. Invite students to share their responses to questions 2 and 3. As they do so, record the answers in two columns on the board

C. Ask students to connect the needs from the first column with the concrete acts in the second column (e.g., the need for food; soup kitchen).

D. Transition the conversation toward why we act charitably. Students may suggest that they would do unto others as they would have done unto them.

Lesson/Activity   *30 minutes*

A. Distribute **Note-Taking Aid.**

B. Read Matthew 25:31-46.

C. Discuss how since Jesus is in each person, and when we help or do not help someone, we are helping or ignoring Christ.

D. Students list the seven Corporal Works of Mercy on their papers:

- Feed the hungry
- Give drink to the thirsty
- Clothe the naked
- Shelter the homeless
- Visit the sick
- Visit the imprisoned
- Bury the dead

E. Discuss that Jesus not only stated the works of mercy, but also provided examples by doing them Himself. Model looking up a Scripture passage, reading it, and identifying which Corporal Work of Mercy is illustrated.

   › Passage: Mark 5:22-24, 35-42 or Luke 8:41-42, 49-55

   › Summary: Jesus comforts Jarius and his family.

   › Work: Bury the dead (which also includes consoling the living).

F. Distribute one of the three "Christ Our Teacher" assignment sheets to students to complete independently. (*Note: Version 3 is most challenging.*) Circulate through the room to offer assistance with looking up and interpreting passages.

G. Select students to share their responses with the class – summarize the passage and identify the corporal work of mercy

Wrap-Up

10 minutes

A. Ask students how the Corporal Works of Mercy from Scripture connected to their responses from the "Coming Home" story.

B. Have students write a corporal act of mercy on an index card and 2-3 ways in which they can live out that act in their community.

Extension Option

Send home the following note:

Dear parents,

Your child has identified a corporal act of mercy to carry out in his/her community. Please help your child to accomplish this goal or another act of mercy and talk about the experience. Then, help your child think of some other ways in which he or she might perform corporal acts of mercy in your neighborhood and parish community.

Enrichment Activity

As a class reread Mathew 5:3-11 and discuss each beatitude. Have students read the **Enrichment Essay: Jesus Teaches Us How to Live** and complete **Handout C: Living the Values of the Kingdom of God** individually or in small groups. Next, randomly give each group one beatitude to consider. Distribute **Handout D: Living Like Christ** and explain the following directions:

➤ On one left side, students should find an example of how Christ realizes one of the Beatitudes in the Bible and quickly create a sketch of that Gospel scene. At the top of that half of the paper they should write a sentence that describes that scene and quote the chapter and verse.

➤ On the right side, students should sketch a scene from their life that demonstrates how they can live the values of the Kingdom of God in imitation of Christ today. Students should write one sentence at the top of the paper that describes the sketch and explains how it shows them living the beatitude.

➤ For a thorough examination of examples of Christ living the Beatitudes in scripture, see the answer key to "Who Are the Blessed?" on page 184.

Bulletin Board Extensions

A. As a class, identify a corporal act of mercy students could complete that would engage the whole class or school (e.g. a food or clothing drive, illustrating place mats for a nursing home, or assembling kits for a homeless shelter). The bulletin board would provide information about the agency or people served as well as how students might participate in this event.

B. Students select one of the Scripture passages that they read and illustrate it. Above the image, students should write the Scripture reference. Beneath the image, students should summarize the Scripture passage and identify the corporal work of mercy. Alternatively, students might find a portrayal of their selected Biblical passage in a work of fine art that could be displayed with their commentary – creating a gallery of sorts.

Hunter's Story—"Coming Home"

Directions: Read the passage and answer the questions below.

Hurricane Katrina struck Biloxi, Mississippi on Monday, August 29, 2005. Before it hit, our family decided to pack up some things and leave to stay with relatives away from the coast. When we left our house, the water was already covering the street. We didn't think the water would rise any higher – it hadn't ever in history. We were wrong.

After the storm, my mom and dad and I returned home to the back bay in Biloxi. As we drove down the streets, we saw houses pulled off their foundations and fishing boats sitting in trees. I heard that my school downtown had been flooded with over 17 feet of water and would not be able to reopen. As we pulled into our neighborhood, my house looked almost perfect. A window had blown out in the front. Had we been spared the worst?

I hopped out of our Jeep, my dog, JP, trailing close behind me. We walked through our yard to get out of the hot sun. As I opened the door to our home, it was clear that my life had changed forever. During the storm, several feet of muddy water had filled the entire house, destroying nearly everything. As the water left the house, it dragged all our clothes, photographs, and furniture out with it. We found some things in our backyard or at the bottom of the canal that ran behind our house. The items were too broken to be worth saving. Most of our things were lost forever.

In the weeks that followed, we worked from sunup to sundown in extreme heat emptying our house of the muck and debris. For about two weeks, there was no electricity, and it was even longer before we had running water. The government made everyone live under a curfew because without lights on the streets — and with most streets filled with wrecked homes and businesses — it was too dangerous to drive anywhere.

Wallowing in pity was not an option. You have to want to help yourself get back up. I didn't have time to think about anything else. Life moved pretty fast after that.

Questions

1. What happened to Hunter's home?
2. What does Hunter need?
3. How could someone answer those needs?

Note-Taking Aide

Directions: In Matthew's Gospel, Christ lists the works of mercy that are expected of us as Christians.

Corporal Works of Mercy

_____

_____

_____

_____

_____

_____

_____

_____

_____

Matthew 25:40
Amen I say to you, whatever you did for one of these least brothers of mine, you did for me.

2 Thessalonians 3:13
But you, brothers, do not be remiss in doing good.

Christ Our Teacher

■ ■

Teacher Note: Differentiate the lesson by offering different versions to different students. Version 3 is more challenging than versions 1 and 2.

1

Directions

1. Look up the Bible passage and read it.
2. Write a 2-3 sentence summary of the passage.
3. Identify the corporal work of mercy referenced in the passage.

Passages

A. Luke 18:35-43 _____

B. Matthew 14:15-21 _____

2

Directions

1. Look up the Bible passage and read it.

2. Write a 2-3 sentence summary of the passage.

3. Identify the corporal work of mercy referenced in the passage.

Passages

A. Luke 10:29-37 _____

B. Matthew 8:1-3 _____

3

Directions

1. Look up the Bible passage and read it.

2. Write a 2-3 sentence summary of the passage.

3. Identify the corporal work of mercy referenced in the passage.

Passages

A. Mark 5:2-15 _____

B. John 8:1-11 _____

Jesus Teaches Us How to Live

Jesus completely and perfectly realized the Beatitudes during his earthly ministry. The purpose of the Beatitudes is to teach us how to be like Christ and in our relationships with other people. The Beatitudes orient us to our ultimate happiness which is life with the Blessed Trinity in Heaven, the Beatific Vision. They make us "partakers of the divine nature and of eternal life" (CCC 1721).

The *Catechism* states that "the Beatitudes depict the countenance of Jesus Christ and portray his charity" (CCC 1717). As guides for how we should be like Christ, the Beatitudes describe how Jesus lived. Jesus, in an act of great charity, modeled for us the ideal Christian life. He asks nothing from us that He has not already done, and he asks us to do what he has done by giving us the Beatitudes. Our response to His charity is to imitate Jesus with the guidance of his Beatitudes. Examining the Scriptures will show us how Jesus lived the Beatitudes and how we can too.

The first beatitude states: **"Blessed are the poor in spirit: for theirs is the kingdom of heaven"** (Matthew 5:3). Jesus exemplifies being poor by remaining completely detached from earthly things and being reliant upon the Father. Many people identify with Jesus because He lives as they do — a life without material possessions. Jesus' words are also about being completely dependent on God. Jesus demonstrates this beatitude in his agony in

the Garden when, he asks, "My Father, if it is not possible that this cup pass without my drinking it, your will be done!" (Matthew 26:42). Jesus does not pridefully assert his own wishes. Rather He humbles himself to the Father's will and so wins for all of us the Kingdom of Heaven. If we humbly recognize that we are God's poor servants, that all our possessions are gifts from God, and that we are dependent on God for every minute of our lives, we will enter His Kingdom.

The second beatitude is: **"Blessed are they who mourn: for they shall be comforted"** (Matthew 5:4). We mourn for what we lack; we weep for what we had and is now gone. Jesus mourned when his friend Lazarus died. Lazarus' sister Martha came to Jesus, saying, "Even now I know that whatever you ask of God, God will give you. I know he [Lazarus] will rise, in the resurrection on the last day. I have come to believe that you are the Messiah, the Son of God" (John 11:22, 24, 27). Even as she grieved, Martha believed in Jesus, and her faith kept her strong. Jesus raised Lazarus from the dead to show us that resurrection is in Jesus, and we will rise at the last day in Jesus. Belief in Jesus and in the eternal life He gives comforts us and strengthens us when we grieve. God blesses us when, even as we mourn for what we have lost, we believe in Jesus and long for the coming of the Kingdom in its fullness.

In the third beatitude, Jesus teaches us: "Blessed are the meek for they will inherit the land" (Matthew 5:5). The word meek does not mean weak. To be meek is to be gentle, humble, teachable, and patient while bearing wrongs. Jesus tells us that he is meek: "learn from me, for I am meek and humble of heart" (Matthew 11:29). Jesus demonstrates his meekness throughout his Passion. Jesus endured beatings, whippings, false accusations, and ridicule with quiet strength, never losing His temper or striking back, never retaliating or resisting. He is firm in doing the will of the Father. Always pointing to the will of the Father and not His own, Jesus willingly demonstrates the ultimate expression of meekness and humility on the Cross. Saint Paul states: "he humbled himself, becoming obedient to death, even death on the cross" (Philippians 2:8). By meekly doing his Father's will, Jesus redeemed the earth. If we imitate Christ by meekly doing God's will, if we control our tempers and submit ourselves to God, then God will bless us by working out our earthly affairs for our good and by giving us our earthly bodies, resurrected and glorified, on the Last Day.

The fourth beatitude tells us: **"Blessed are they who hunger and thirst for righteousness, for they will be satisfied"** (Matthew 5:6). We all hunger and thirst for food and drink because our bodies need these things. In this beatitude, Jesus re-orients our attention to something we ought even more deeply to hunger and thirst for: righteousness. Jesus miraculously fed five thousand people to care for their physical needs. He also taught them with his words and example, in order to awaken in them an awareness of their spiritual need for righteousness. Jesus, in his perfect relationship with the Father, is perfect

righteousness. Jesus wants us to hunger for righteousness, so that He can satisfy our hunger by giving us Himself.

The fifth beatitude states: **"Blessed are the merciful, for they will be shown mercy"** (Matthew 5:7). Mercy is love that keeps on loving after it has been rejected. Jesus' life fully reveals that God's love is complete mercy. Jesus demonstrates throughout the Gospels how to be merciful. When Pharisees caught a woman in adultery and wanted to stone her, Jesus sent them away and forgave the woman. Jesus teaches us to forgive each other when we pray to the Father: "Forgive us our debts, as we forgive our debtors" (Matthew 6:12). Jesus shares three parables in Luke 15 that demonstrate how God longs to show mercy to us if we ask for it: "There will be more joy in heaven over one sinner who repents than over ninety-nine righteous people who have no need of repentance" (Luke 15:7). For God's mercy not only forgives sin, He also rejoices when the sinner returns. And since we all need God's mercy, we must show mercy to each other. God will rejoice when we come to Him, and He will welcome us into Heaven.

"Blessed are the clean of heart, for they will see God," is the sixth beatitude. This beatitude shows us the connection between our minds, bodies, and souls. Jesus' mind, body, and soul were clean, for He lived a sinless life, and He approached everyone with pure intentions and charity in His heart. Jesus exemplified having a clean heart when He called Zacchaeus to come to Him. Zacchaeus was rich, because even though he was a Jew, he worked for the Romans as a tax collector. He often forced people to pay more in taxes than they owed. Jesus, because He had a clean heart, could perceive that Zacchaeus wanted to change. Zacchaeus indeed wanted to change so much that when Jesus called him, Zacchaeus ran to Jesus, and greeted Him with joy, saying, "half of my possessions, Lord, I shall give to the poor, and if I have extorted anything from anyone I shall repay it four times over" (Luke 19:8). For when Zacchaeus welcomed Jesus with joy, his heart grew so clean that he saw that Jesus is God, and he promised to change his life. Like Zacchaeus, we must strive and pray to cleanse ourselves of sin so that we can see God. Our hearts first become clean when Jesus calls us to come to Him, through baptism, to become His adopted sons and daughters. Jesus wants us to have clean hearts, and minds, bodies, and souls, so that He can redeem us. Jesus said to Zacchaeus, "today salvation has come to this house. For the Son of Man has come to seek and to save" (Luke 19:9-10). Jesus seeks us to save us, so that we can all see Him for eternity.

In the seventh beatitude, Jesus teaches us: **"Blessed are the peacemakers, for they will be called the children of God"** (Matthew 5:9). Jesus lives out this beatitude in His incarnation: He became man to reconcile us to the Father so that we can be the sons and daughters of God. Jesus advises us to resolve arguments with each other before offering our prayers to God: "Leave your gift there at the altar, go first and be reconciled with your brother, and then come and offer your gift" (Matthew 5:24). As the perfect example of peacemaking, Jesus forgives Peter for denying him (John 21:15-19). Moreover, before offering Himself to the Father on the

Cross, Jesus wanted to make peace with the people who had crucified him; he pleaded for them: "Father, forgive them, they know not what they do" (Luke 23:34). If we strive for peace, then we are imitating the Son of God, and we will live in God's love for us as his sons and daughters.

The final beatitude states: **"Blessed are they who are persecuted for the sake of righteousness, for theirs is the kingdom of heaven"** (Matthew 5:10). Jesus endured insults, false accusations, persecution, insistent questioning, plots of entrapment, and death, all so that we may join him in the kingdom of heaven. When Christ was dying on the cross, two criminals were also crucified, one on either side of Jesus. One of these men mocked Jesus. The other man risked also being mocked, for he chose to believe in Jesus. He said to Jesus, "Jesus, remember me when you come into your kingdom" (Luke 23:42). Jesus answered and promised him, "Amen, I say to you, today you will be with me in Paradise" (Luke 23:43). When we suffer, especially for Jesus, we can grow strong in love for Him to be with Him for eternity.

Jesus' life is the Beatitudes lived out in reality. We can also live according to the Beatitudes by following Christ. As Jesus taught the Ancient Jews that the Beatitudes fulfilled the Old Testament promises, Jesus teaches us that the Beatitudes are our tools for living in the light of Christ despite modern society's malformed values. In each beatitude, Jesus promises us something. If we live according to the Beatitudes, Jesus will bless us by fulfilling His promises: by bringing us into his Kingdom.

Living the Values of the Kingdom of God

Beatitude	Example of how to live the value(s) expressed in the beatitude	Examples of values that are opposite of those expressed in the beatitude
Blessed are the poor in spirit.		
Blessed are they who mourn.		
Blessed are the meek.		
Blessed are the merciful.		
Blessed are those who hunger and thirst for righteousness.		
Blessed are the pure in heart.		
Blessed are the peacemakers.		
Blessed are those who are persecuted for righteousness' sake.		

Living Like Christ

Beatitude: _____

Sketch a Gospel scene that shows Christ living this beatitude:	Sketch a scene from your life that shows you living this beatitude:
Describe the scene and note the chapter and verse that this scene depicts:	Describe the scene and explain why you drew the image you did:

Answer Key

Sacred Art and the Beatitudes: Jesus Teaches Us How to Live

1. Jesus, the Apostles Peter, James, and John; Moses, Elijah, the Virgin Mary, St. Dominic. The fresco depicts the Transfiguration.

2. Accept reasoned answers.

3. Glorified, triumphant, beautiful, illuminated, bright, etc. He is standing on a rock.

4. Accept reasoned answers.

5. Accept reasoned answers, telling students if necessary that the artist was not aiming at a historical representation of the Transfiguration, but rather a depiction that would be spiritually meaningful.

6. They were so surprised and scared that they fell down. Jesus told them not to be afraid.

7. The fresco reminds us that Jesus has already won the Kingdom for us. We will have struggles in this world, but he has overcome death. Like His Body was transfigured and glorified, He will give us our bodies, resurrected and glorified, on the Last Day.

8. Accept reasoned answers.

Handout A: Coming Home

1. Hunter's home was destroyed by the hurricane, and he lost everything.

2. Hunter needs shelter, clothing, food, and drink.

3. Students might offer: a refugee center, a soup kitchen, or a food bank, or people might donate food, clothing, money, and their own service to support agencies or provide direct assistance.

Handout B: Christ: Our Teacher

Version 1

A. Luke 18: 35-43: Visit the sick. Jesus speaks with a blind beggar even though others ignore the man. Jesus heals the beggar of his blindness.

B. Matthew 14:15-21: Feed the hungry. Jesus had many people following him, and they are growing hungry. Jesus provides food for them in the miracle of the loaves and fishes.

Version 2

A. Luke 10: 29-37: Shelter the homeless; also, visit the sick, feed the hungry. In the parable of the good Samaritan, the Samaritan helps the man and brings him to an inn to care for him when others would not do so.

B. Matthew 8: 1-3: Visit the sick. Jesus was asked to heal a leper. Jesus did so when others in His society would not even consider touching someone with leprosy.

Version 3

A. Mark 5: 2-15: Visit the sick. Jesus visits the sick—in this case someone who is mentally ill and possessed by demons. Christ offers comfort to him and heals him of his affliction.

B. John 8: 1-11: Visit the imprisoned. A woman has broken a law and is condemned to death. Jesus forgives her and asks her accusers if they have ever committed a sin.

The Beatitudes and Moral Choices

Overview

Jesus' central moral discourse begins with those famous paradoxical promises, the Beatitudes, directing the human pursuit of happiness. In the modern era, many have come to view the world as a subjective assembly of events and ideas in which there is no universal or objective reality, and happiness has been relegated to the eyes of the beholder. But happiness is not simply a sentiment; instead, happiness is a conscious decision to will the good of the other over self. Jesus' love is demonstrated in this: "I have told you this so that my joy may be in you and your joy may be complete. This is my commandment: love one another as I love you. No one has greater love than this, to lay down one's life for one's friends."

Grade Level

 HS

Time

One fifty-minute class

Connection to the Catechism

> CCC 580
> CCC 1716
> CCC 1722
> CCC 1723
> CCC 2053

Essential Questions

> Are happiness and goodness different? Are they compatible?
> Is Christianity simply a religion that aims to help individuals justify sadness, rejection, and injustice?
> Why is the human heart the central battleground between good and evil?
> What did Jesus do to become victorious, and how is that victory ongoing?

BIBLICAL TOUCHSTONES

Do not think that I have come to abolish the law or the prophets. I have come not to abolish but to fulfill.

MATTHEW 5:17

Love does no evil to the neighbor; hence, love is the fulfillment of the law.

ROMANS 13:10

The Last Judgment

BY MICHELANGELO BUONARROTI (C. 1536-1541)

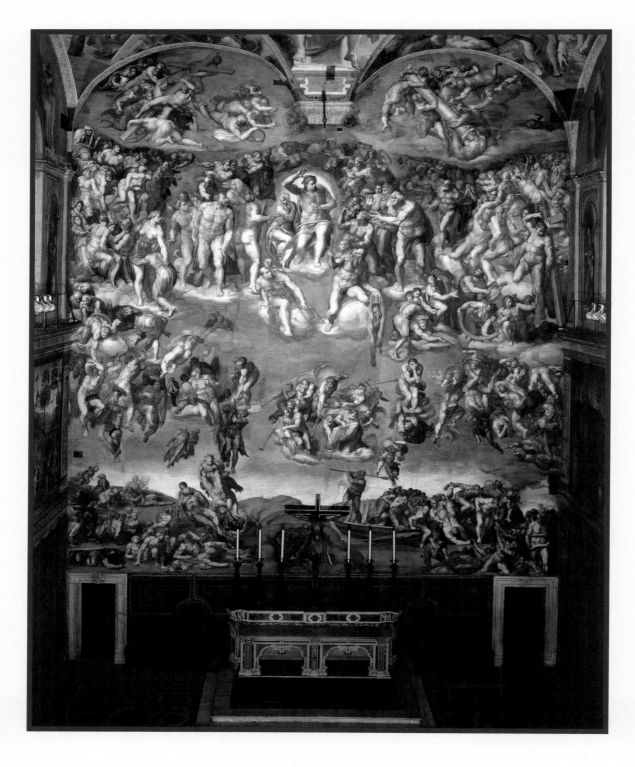

Michelangelo Buonarroti, *The Last Judgment* (1536-1541), fresco,
Sistine Chapel, Apostolic Palace, Vatican City.

Sacred Art and the Beatitudes
The Beatitudes and Moral Choices

 The Last Judgment, by Michelangelo Buonarroti (c. 1536-1541)

Directions: Take some time to quietly view and reflect on the art. Let yourself be inspired in any way that happens naturally. Then think about the questions below, and discuss them with your classmates.

Conversation Questions

1. Where can you see this work of art? How long did it take Michelangelo to complete it?

2. Who is the central figure of this masterpiece? What does He seem to be doing with His hands?

3. What is the main contrast you see in this fresco? What are the two kinds of souls, and what is happening to them?

4. Is it possible to understand some truth from this painting even without knowing who all the people are, or what exactly is happening in every part of the painting? If so, what is that truth?

5. This fresco is on the altar wall of the Sistine Chapel. It is huge — 44 feet by 39 feet, or almost four stories tall. Imagine yourself viewing it in real life, amid the incense, candles, and softly murmured prayers in the chapel. How do you think the scale of the work of art would affect you?

6. The walls and ceiling of the Sistine Chapel are almost entirely covered with beautiful frescoes. You have to crane your neck to see all of them, and even use binoculars to see all the details. They took many years to complete at great expense. Why would the Church go through all that trouble?

7. Look for figures/scenes including the ones below. How do they add to the meaning of this work?

    ›   The Virgin Mary
    ›   Sts. Peter and Paul
    ›   Scenes from Christ's Passion
    ›   Charon
    ›   King Minos

Lesson Plan

Materials

- Background Essay: The Beatitudes and Moral Choices
- Handout A: Statements from the Sermon on the Mount.

Background/Homework

Read the **Background Essay** and answer the questions.

Warm-Up   *15 minutes*

A. Read aloud together paragraphs 1716, 1722, and 1723 from the *Catechism of the Catholic Church*, and/or Psalm 51.

B. Write the following questions on the board, and have students choose one and write a brief journal response.

   - What is the Christian portrait or ultimate illustration of happiness?

   - Are happiness and goodness different? Are they compatible?

   - How did the Old Law prepare the way for the New Law?

   - Did the New Law eradicate or abolish the Old Law? Or, does the New Law perfect and complete the Old Law?

C. Ask a few students to share their responses, and lead discussion toward the way Jesus fulfills and perfects the Old Law. "In Jesus, the Law no longer appears engraved on tables of stone but 'upon the heart' of the Servant who becomes 'a covenant to the people,' because he will 'faithfully bring forth justice'" (CCC 580).

Activity

A. Distribute **Handout A: Statements from the Sermon on the Mount**. Have students complete it individually or in pairs. Reconvene the class for students to share responses.

Discussion Questions

›   What is the connection between the Beatitudes and the Crucifixion?

›   Why does the Crucifixion illustrate true joy?

›   Why are the Beatitudes more realistic than unrealistic?

›   Is Christianity simply a religion that aims to help individuals justify sadness, rejection, and injustice?

›   Is non-violence the only answer to injustice?

›   Why is the human heart the central battleground between good and evil? What did Jesus do to become victorious, and how is that victory ongoing?

Wrap-Up

Ask groups to write down 3 summary statements based on the classroom activities and discussion, and share them with the class. Statements should capture the idea that in Jesus Christ, love is the fulfillment of the law.

Enrichment Option

St. Ireneus pronounced, "The glory of God is a human being fully alive." Have students write a 100-word essay in response to the questions: Is it impossible or unrealistic to live out the Beatitudes in order to pursue true goodness? Student responses should mention at least 3 of the main ideas discussed in the lesson.

The Beatitudes and Moral Choices

In December of 2006, Will Smith starred in a film he co-produced entitled "The Pursuit of Happyness." Chris Garnder (Will Smith), a San Franciscan salesman, struggles mightily to support his son. His girlfriend abruptly leaves, and shortly thereafter Chris and his son Christopher Jr. (Jaden Smith) are evicted from their apartment. Chris cannot find meaningful or financially stable employment, leaving him and his son to stay in homeless shelters and eventually in the bathroom of a metro station. He ultimately lands a position as an intern at a highly competitive stockbroker firm, although still receiving no compensation or salary. Chris rises to become a Wall Street legend but not before he faces losing everything, including his beloved and trusting son.

We Are Hard-Wired for Inward Joy

There is an element of the plot line that is universally and inherently attractive to the human spirit. A father nearly forfeits every material achievement to build a stable foundation for his family. He unexpectedly pursues a seemingly senseless unpaid internship just so he can crack a door that could potentially open to lasting financial security. In the process, the father descends to such a deprived worldly position that he cannot even provide a roof for his son. Setback after setback, and the father never loses sight of the prize: happiness for his son. The unconditional

The Transfiguration, Raphael.

love shared between the two is the only source of hope as they search for a snippet of steadiness.

The movie wrenches the human heart for all of the aforementioned reasons. But why are humans naturally attracted to stories that illustrate sacrifice and the relentless search for joy? Why does the life of Chris Gardner tug at the very core of the human person? How is it that so-called success stories are more appealing when suffering is co-mingled with absolute love, even when the suffering experienced is the direct result of an almost inescapable injustice? Maybe Jesus wasn't totally off his rocker when he stated, "Blessed are the poor in spirit, for theirs is the kingdom of heaven." The radicalism of the beatitudes isn't so impossible if we consider the intrigue and unmistakable attractiveness of Chris Gardner. The human person is in fact hard-wired for inward joy, and even though injustices forever impede our path toward lasting happiness, life is worth living and the pursuit remains possible.

Jesus did not simply preach, "Do unto others as you would have them do unto you." It is commonplace for moderns to reduce morality to an absolute rule or universal principle that can be applied at all times. It is equally as common for moderns to believe that "it depends on the situation" or "to each his own." Many try to pull out from Jesus' teachings those sayings or ideas that are generally regarded being as a shared belief amongst all cultures (even if they are not). Jesus as a radical is pushed aside; moreover, Jesus as the Word of God, the second person of Trinity, and the divine Godhead made manifest is almost forgotten. Why is the identity of Jesus reduced to one man among many? Because if Jesus is God, then everything He ever did or said holds decisive implications for the human person. His commandments are more than suggestions.

The Beatitudes and the Old Testament

Key to understanding those commandments is the Old Testament.

Moses was called to be God's chosen instrument to liberate the Israelites from slavery. Shortly after departing Egypt, Moses ascends Mt. Sinai; there God decides to enter into a unique covenant with the people of Israel. Now that the Israelites were free, God anticipated the need for direction, purpose, and security from false influences. Thus, Moses descended the mountain prepared to finalize the covenant between God and Israel; but first, the Israelites had to consent to God's plan.

The Ten Commandments were given to Moses on top of Mount Sinai. Moses is pictured as a lawgiver, although the directives were received from God. These directives are famously recorded on stone tablets. These biblical motifs are essential if we are to understand Jesus' moral teaching. It is important to note that even though the Ten Commandments are to some extent common sense, the law is still portrayed as existing outside the human person. These simple commands appear as a series of "no," but God just said "yes" by freeing the Israelites. The negative directives are supposed to prevent the Israelites from falling back into slavery by showing them the path towards social harmony and spiritual excellence. But since the law is essentially exterior to the human person, the Israelites perpetually fail to embrace the 'yes'. Written on stone tablets, the Israelites struggle to interiorize the Ten Commandments. Sin pervades the biblical narrative, and the Old Law appears ineffective.

The Old Testament precedent is the key to unlocking the message of the Beatitudes.

According to the gospel of Matthew, Jesus ascends the mountain to speak with both His disciples and the crowds, thereby assuming the position of lawgiver. Different from Moses, Jesus is the ultimate mediator because He is both God and man; He is the Word who spoke the Law into existence, and who invited man into communion by imprinting His image on His greatest creature. The Sermon on the Mount is the promulgation of the New Law. The Beatitudes are paradoxical promises of lasting happiness; these promises coupled with the remainder of the discourse shift the focus away from those stone tablets and toward the human heart. Because sin and injustice are unavoidable, the heart needs supernatural energy to sustain against adversity. The heart is the root of all sin but it is also the gate to goodness.

The Ten Commandments are akin to the minimum rules needed in order to play the game; the beatitudes are the skills required to become an excellently happy, flourishing human. Christian morality cannot be reduced to merely following rules. The rules are there to protect the life-giving relationship that God offers us. Thus, the Christian morality is a radical lifestyle culminating from challenging and selfless choices. "Thus, the last will be first, and the first will be last" (Matthew 20:16). Jesus' radical statements are intended to be a reality check: happiness is maximized by minimizing self; go beyond the minimum and the good will set you free. The example of the saints, especially the martyrs, show us that we too can live the radical life of self-giving love of the Beatitudes.

The Christian Difference

In short, the Christian difference is the revolutionary call to interior joy. Jesus boldly supersedes the Old Law because he can; He is the one who set the ball in motion, first providing the Old Law in order to prepare the human heart for radicalism of the New Law. A clean heart is the root of happiness; moreover, a clean heart is the only true and effective path aimed directly at the good. Jesus' heart was pierced for our offenses; so too the human heart—pursuing happiness is possible when the heart is willing to suffer for others. "Blessed are the pure in heart, for they shall see God" (Matthew 5:8). God chose to be seen on a cross, arms outstretched, as he embraced all of humanity. The good life is the happy life; humanity cannot be excellently joyful without the embrace and support of the God-Savior.

Conversation Questions

1. Can morality be reduced to an absolute rule? Does the individual determine what is right or wrong? Why or why not?

2. Is happiness simply a sentiment that all humans crave and desire? Why or why not?

3. How do the Beatitudes fulfill and complete the Ten Commandments?

Statements from the Sermon on the Mount

The Beatitudes are the central moral teaching of the Christian faith. Although the Ten Commandments may be more familiar to some as the set of moral guidelines, the Beatitudes are distinctively Christian.

"Following Jesus Christ involves keeping the Commandments. The Law has not been abolished, but rather man is invited to rediscover it in the person of his Master who is its perfect fulfillment" (CCC 2053).

Directions: Read each statement and put Jesus' teaching in your own words. How does each statement reflect Jesus' fulfillment of the Old Law?

1. "Do not think that I have come to abolish the law or the prophets. I have come not to abolish but to fulfill. Amen, I say to you, until heaven and earth pass away, not the smallest letter or the smallest part of a letter will pass from the law, until all things have taken place" (Matthew 5:17-18).

   _____

   _____

   _____

   _____

2. "You have heard that it was said to your ancestors, 'You shall not kill; and whoever kills will be liable to judgment.' But I say to you, whoever is angry with his brother will be liable to judgment, and whoever says to his brother, 'Raqa,' will be answerable to the Sanhedrin, and whoever says, 'You fool,' will be liable to fiery Gehenna" (Matthew 5:21-22).

   _____

   _____

   _____

   _____

3. "You have heard that it was said, 'An eye for an eye and a tooth for a tooth.' But I say to you, offer no resistance to one who is evil. When someone strikes you on (your) right cheek, turn the other one to him as well. If anyone wants to go to law with you over your tunic, hand him your cloak as well. Should anyone press you into service for one mile, go with him for two miles. Give to the one who asks of you, and do not turn your back on one who wants to borrow" (Matthew 5:38-42).

_____

_____

_____

_____

4. "You have heard that it was said, 'You shall love your neighbor and hate your enemy.' But I say to you, love your enemies, and pray for those who persecute you, that you may be children of your heavenly Father, for he makes his sun rise on the bad and the good, and causes rain to fall on the just and the unjust. For if you love those who love you, what recompense will you have? Do not the tax collectors do the same? And if you greet your brothers only, what is unusual about that? Do not the pagans do the same? So be perfect, just as your heavenly Father is perfect" (Matthew 5:43-48).

_____

_____

_____

_____

5. "Stop judging, that you may not be judged. For as you judge, so will you be judged, and the measure with which you measure will be measured out to you. Why do you notice the splinter in your brother's eye, but do not perceive the wooden beam in your own eye? How can you say to your brother, 'Let me remove that splinter from your eye,' while the wooden beam is in your eye? You hypocrite, remove the wooden beam from your eye first; then you will see clearly to remove the splinter from your brother's eye" (Matthew 7:2-5).

_____

_____

_____

_____

Answer Key

Sacred Art and the Beatitudes: The Beatitudes and Moral Choices

1. The Sistine Chapel in the Vatican. Five years.

2. Jesus Christ. He has one hand up and the other down.

3. Christ is raising the righteous to heaven with His right hand, and condemning the damned to hell with His left.

4. Yes. The painting depicts a vision of the Last Judgment – Christ judges all of humanity. Accept additional reasoned answers.

5. Accept reasoned answers.

6. The Church has always taken care to create and preserve beautiful works of art that show us the way to the Divine. Fine art can dispose us to what is good, beautiful, and true.

Background Essay

1. It is tempting to try reduce morality to a single, absolute rule, or, on the other hand, to say that there is no such thing as right and wrong. Neither are true. It is true that certain things are always wrong (you may never do evil so that good may result) and some are always good (loving God, loving neighbor). In day-to-day life, morality means seeking Christ, following Him, and conforming your life to Him by keeping His Commandments.

2. No, happiness is not just a "feeling." It comes in being satisfied in our desire to be satisfied. Only God can give us this joy.

3. The Ten Commandments are like the minimum requirement, while the Beatitudes perfect the call to life in Jesus Christ and interior joy.

Handout B: Statements from the Sermon on the Mount

1. Jesus does not come to destroy the Old Law, but to bring it into its full meaning and make it better. The law will endure till the end of time.

2. Refraining from murder is not sufficient. Being angry and unkind to someone is in a way like killing that person. Jesus tells us more about the meaning of this commandment.

3. Retribution or vengeance is not justice. If someone hurts you, you should not try to get back at him or her. Be meek, gentle, and giving. Jesus tells us that we should not expect or want things to be "equal," but rather we should lay down our lives for our loved ones and neighbors.

4. The defining mark of a Christian is not only love of neighbor, but love of enemies. Jesus tells us that there is nothing particularly special about loving our friends – everyone can do that. To love and pray for those who would do us harm is what sets us apart in Jesus Christ.

5. You cannot judge others' hearts. All humans struggle with sin, and to criticize others leads to hypocrisy.

Who Are the Blessed?

Overview

The Beatitudes were part of Jesus' teaching about how we can be perfectly happy, that is, to behold the beatific vision that is God in heaven. This lesson challenges students to understand what Jesus means by "blessed" or "happy," and to investigate Scripture to discover who the blessed are: those who may or may not attain a certain amount of imperfect happiness in their earthly lives, but will most definitely be satisfied and fulfilled by God in Heaven.

Grade Level

 HS

Time

Two to three fifty-minute classes

Connection to the Catechism

- › CCC 1716
- › CCC 1717

Essential Questions

- › What does Jesus mean by "blessed"?
- › What did He mean by words like "poor," "meek," "mourn," "hunger," "thirst," and others?
- › How can I use the whole Bible to uncover the meaning of these words, and start living the Beatitudes myself?

BIBLICAL TOUCHSTONES

God does not see as a mortal, who sees the appearance. The LORD looks into the heart.

1 SAMUEL 16:7

I am the Way, and the Truth, and the Life.

JOHN 14:6

The Anastasis

Apse fresco of the Anastasis, Church of the Holy Saviour in Chora.

Sacred Art and the Beatitudes
Who Are the Blessed?

 The Anastasis, *Church of the Holy Saviour*

Directions: Take some time to quietly view and reflect on the art. Let yourself be inspired in any way that happens naturally. Then think about the questions below, and discuss them with your classmates.

Conversation Questions

1. When you look at this fresco, what do you first notice? What is your favorite part?

2. How would you describe the overall mood of this work of art?

3. Recite the Apostles Creed. What event described in that profession of faith does this fresco depict?

4. Off to the sides are King David, King Solomon, St. John the Baptist, Abel, and others. Who do you think are the two people whom Jesus grasps by the wrists?

5. How would you describe Jesus' posture? What does the artist show us about who Christ is by the way he painted Him?

6. Read Matthew 16:18. What does this fresco teach us about Jesus' promises to all of humanity?

Lesson Plan

Materials

> Background Essay: Who Are the Blessed?

> Handouts A-G: Who Are the Blessed?

> Handout H: Beatitudes Prayer

Background/Homework

Have students read the Background Essay and answer the critical thinking questions. Ask students to come to class prepared to discuss their answers to critical thinking question number 4, specifically, to have a list of 3 or 4 things that our culture today suggests will make us happy.

Warm-Up
20 minutes

A. Show the music video for the song "Happy" by Pharrell Williams, or, if that's not possible, play an audio recording of the song. Distribute or project a copy of the lyrics to the song.

B. Ask a few students to share some things that make them happy. Accept any answers that are reasonable and appropriate. Keep a brainstorm list on the board.

> Ask/discuss: Why do these things make you happy? How long does that happiness last?

C. Ask a few students to share some items from their list of 3 or 4 things that our culture today suggests will make us happy. Accept any answers that are reasonable and appropriate. Keep a brainstorm list on the board.

> Ask/discuss: How long does the happiness these things provide last? Why do you think we settle for less when we want so much more?

D. Write the words "Perfect Happiness" and "Imperfect Happiness" on the board. Ask for students to define the terms and write the definitions on the board.

> ▸ Ask/discuss: In the song "Happy" by Pharrell Williams, do you think you he is singing about imperfect or perfect happiness? Why do you think so?
>
> *Students may answer with one or the other, but the important thing is that they provide evidence from the song. One could argue that at times he is singing about both.*

E. Explain: The Beatitudes were part of Jesus' teaching about how we can be perfectly happy, that is, to behold the beatific vision that is God in heaven. This, of course, will come after our earthly life. In order to get to heaven, we must have faith and keep the Lord's commandments. Jesus teaches those who are poor, those who mourn or weep, those who are meek, those who hunger and thirst for righteousness, those who are merciful, those who are clean of heart, those who are peacemakers, and those who are persecuted for the sake of righteousness, are those who may or may not attain a certain amount of imperfect happiness in their earthly lives, but will most definitely be satisfied and fulfilled by God in Heaven.

Activity   *1-2 class periods*

A. Distribute **Handouts A-G: Who Are the Blessed?**

B. Explain: In our consideration of the Beatitudes and happiness, it is important for us to consider who it is exactly that Jesus proclaimed to be "blessed" or "happy." We must also consider how Jesus, who is our perfect model of holiness, exemplified each beatitude. Lastly, we need to consider what each beatitude is calling us to do in our own lives in order to be "blessed."

C. First, divide students into eight groups. Assign each group to work on one of the Handouts. Have each group look up the given Scripture passages together and then discuss their findings. Then have students record a brief note summarizing each passage in the space provided, paying particular attention to what the passage has to say about the topic heading (to whom the beatitude is referring, how Jesus exemplifies the beatitude, or what the beatitude is calling us to do).

   Note: You may want to do one of the beatitudes with the entire class as an example. In that case, divide students into seven groups and proceed as described.

D. Next, have students individually write a 3-5 sentence summary statement that fully and accurately summarizes what they have learned from the Scripture passages within the three given topics.

E. Lastly, have students jigsaw into new groups in which each person studied a different beatitude. Have students share their findings with each other. Direct students to take notes about their new learning on each beatitude either in their own notebooks/ journals or fill out **Handouts A-G.**

F. Move around the classroom monitoring discussions and entering into various small group conversations as necessary.

G. Lastly, have each group share their findings. Engage in large group discussion with the students, writing key points on the board. Direct students to take notes on each beatitude.

Wrap-Up   *15 minutes*

A. Distribute **Handout H: Beatitudes Prayer**.

B. Have each beatitude group write a prayer petition based upon their assigned beatitude to be shared with the rest of class in a mini prayer service at the end of the lesson.

C. Each prayer petition should be formatted as following:

> First, read the assigned beatitude.

> Then, offer a statement of thanksgiving.

> Next, make a statement of asking or petition.

> Close with, "We pray to the Lord," to which all respond, "Lord, hear our prayer."

An example:

Beatitudes	Petitions
"Blessed are the poor in spirit, for theirs is the kingdom of heaven." –Matthew 5:3	Thanksgiving: **Lord, we thank you for**... all the good things you have given to us, all of our possessions, our homes, the food we eat, and our family and friends. Asking/Petition: **We ask, Lord**... that you give us the desire to live simply and in a spirit of poverty, so that we can be with you in your Kingdom. **We pray to the Lord ... Lord, hear our prayer.**

Extension Options

A. Instead of dividing students into groups and treating this as one lesson, have every student do every beatitude and treat this as a whole unit of study.

B. Have students search for and add their own Scripture passages to the activity. For example, "Blessed are the poor in spirit," on top of looking up the given Scripture passages that speak to the meaning of who is "poor in spirit," students can find a Scripture passage on their own that speaks to the meaning of the phrase, and add it to the list. This could be done for each category and each beatitude.

Who Are the Blessed?

Both Matthew and Luke include the story of the Beatitudes in their Gospels. Matthew depicts Jesus delivering eight Beatitudes in a sermon on a mountain, while Luke depicts Jesus delivering only four Beatitudes in a sermon on a plain. The four Beatitudes that Luke writes about parallel four of the Beatitudes Matthew includes, while using slightly different language. These differences in language can help to deepen our understanding of what Jesus meant by each teaching.

All Saints, Bl. Fra Angelico

You Were Created for Happiness

In both Matthew and Luke, Jesus begins each Beatitude with the saying, "Blessed are …," and then continues each statement with a teaching on who is "blessed" and what their "reward" will be for their blessedness. Some translations of Scripture use the phrase "Happy are …" instead, though the meaning is the same. It is helpful to consider in more detail what Jesus meant when he said "blessed" or "happy" so that we can more fully understand the meaning of the Beatitudes. In fact, Jesus' understanding of being "blessed" or "happiness" was very different from the typical understanding of the words today. It is common today for people to talk about doing whatever makes them happy or similarly to encounter the hashtag *#blessed* on social media. In both situations, the words are most likely being used to express the feeling or emotion of *pleasure*, or the

feeling or emotion of being *fortunate*. In both cases, the happiness or blessedness that is experienced is something that is temporary and fleeting, as all feelings and emotions are. The blessedness and happiness that Jesus had in mind, was something very different, something much closer in meaning to the classical philosophical definition of happiness.

St. Augustine writes, "All men agree in desiring the last end, which is happiness." By "last end," St. Augustine means "purpose." In other words, Augustine is saying that all men desire to achieve their purpose, which is happiness. St. Thomas Aquinas furthers this idea, writing, "to desire happiness is nothing else than to desire that one's will be satisfied." Many things in our earthly lives can bring us temporary pleasure, but nothing can fully satisfy our desire to *be satisfied*, or to be fulfilled. Aquinas calls the temporary pleasure that comes from earthly goods an imperfect happiness. Perfect happiness, or blessedness, will only be achieved when we behold the beatific vision of God in heaven, who is all good and perfect. St. Augustine famously writes of this perfect satisfaction in God: "Our hearts are restless until they rest in you." He understood that only the infinite God satisfies infinitely.

Imperfect vs. Perfect Happiness

God allows us a preview of the perfect happiness that awaits us in heaven when we experience an imperfect happiness here on earth. Jesus, in speaking of the model of holiness he has given to us, said, "If you understand this, blessed are you if you do it." Jesus is referring to both faith and works, what we *know* and what we *do*, as a means to achieve some imperfect happiness here on earth as well as our perfect happiness in heaven. Aquinas, of course, agrees with Jesus, and writes, "happiness is the reward of works and virtue." This understanding of happiness, we can conclude, is likely closer to what Jesus means by "Blessed are ..." or "Happy are ..." than the *#blessed* of social media, or the temporary pleasure our modern world describes as happiness. In other words, in the Beatitudes, we can understand Jesus to be saying that those who are poor, those who mourn or weep, those who are meek, those who hunger and thirst for righteousness, those who are merciful, those who are clean of heart, those who are peacemakers, and those who are persecuted for the sake of righteousness, are those who may or may not attain a certain amount of imperfect happiness in their earthly lives, but will most definitely be satisfied and fulfilled by God in heaven.

Comprehension and Critical Thinking Questions

1. Why do you think Jesus might have had a standard message that He used when He taught in the various places He went?

2. What is the difference between the typical modern definition of happiness or being blessed and the classical, philosophical definition of happiness or being blessed?

3. What is imperfect happiness? What is perfect happiness? Which was Jesus referring to in the Beatitudes?

4. What are 3-4 things that our culture today suggests will make us happy? Why do you think we so easily settle for temporary pleasure when we all desire the satisfaction of perfect happiness?

Who Are the Blessed?

> **"Blessed are the poor in spirit, for theirs is the kingdom of Heaven."**
> —Matthew 5:3

Who are the "poor in spirit"?

A. James 2:5

_____

_____

_____

B. 2 Corinthians 6:10

_____

_____

_____

How is Jesus "poor"?

A. 2 Corinthians 8:9

_____

_____

_____

B. Three Kinds of Poverty

1. _____

   a. Luke 2:7

      _____

      _____

      _____

   b. Luke 2:22-24

      _____

      _____

      _____

   c. Leviticus 12:8

      _____

      _____

      _____

2. _____

   a. Matthew 10:37

      _____

      _____

      _____

   b. Matthew 12:46-50

      _____

      _____

      _____

   c. Luke 23: 44-49

      _____

      _____

      _____

3. _____

   a. John 18:33-37

   _____

   _____

   _____

   b. Matthew 4:8-10

   _____

   _____

   _____

   c. Philippians 2:6-7

   _____

   _____

   _____

What does this beatitude call us to do?

A. Matthew 19:16-22

   _____

   _____

   _____

B. Matthew 18:8-9

   _____

   _____

   _____

Four Evangelists, Jacob Jordaens

Summary Statement

Who Are the Blessed?

> **"Blessed are they who mourn [now weeping],**
> **for they will be comforted."** — Matthew 5:4

Who are those who "mourn" or "weep"?

A. Romans 8:19-23

_____

_____

_____

B. Matthew 26:74-75

_____

_____

_____

C. Romans 12:15

_____

_____

D. Psalm 137:1-4

_____

_____

_____

E. Psalm 42:3, 10

_____

_____

_____

How does Jesus "mourn" or "weep"?

A. Hebrews 12:2

_____

_____

_____

B. John 11:32-35

_____

_____

_____

What does this beatitude call us to do?

A. Hebrews 12:1-3

_____

_____

_____

B. 1 Peter 4:12-14

_____

_____

_____

The Raising of Lazarus, Duccio

C. Psalm 71:23

_____

_____

_____

D. 1 Peter 3:15

_____

_____

_____

Summary Statement

Who Are the Blessed?

"Blessed are the meek, for they will inherit the land." –Matthew 5:5

Who are the "meek"?

A. Mark 9:35

_____

_____

_____

B. Proverbs 15:1

_____

_____

_____

C. Proverbs 15:4

_____

_____

_____

D. Sirach 6:5

_____

_____

_____

How is Jesus "meek"?

A. Matthew 11:29

_____

_____

_____

B. John 13:1-17

_____

_____

_____

C. 1 Peter 2:23

_____

_____

_____

D. Matthew 21:1-9

_____

_____

_____

What does this beatitude call us to do?

A. 1 Peter 3:15

_____

_____

_____

B. Matthew 16:24

_____

_____

_____

C. Galatians 5:22-26

_____

_____

_____

D. 1 Colossians 3:12

_____

_____

_____

The Arrest of Christ, The Master of the Evora

Summary Statement

Who Are the Blessed?

"Blessed are they who hunger and thirst for righteousness,
for they will be satisfied." —Matthew 5:6

Who are the "hungry and thirsty"?

A. Luke 1:53

_____

_____

_____

B. Luke 6:25

_____

_____

_____

C. Luke 12:34

_____

_____

_____

How does Jesus "satisfy"?

A. John 6:35, 53-58

_____

_____

_____

B. John 4:13-15

_____

_____

_____

C. 1 Peter 2:21

_____

_____

_____

The Last Supper, Juan de Juanes

What does this beatitude call us to do?

A. Matthew 22:37-40

_____

_____

_____

B. Matthew 25:31-46

_____

_____

_____

Summary Statement

Who Are the Blessed?

■

"Blessed are the merciful, for they will be shown mercy." —Matthew 5:7

Who are the "merciful"?

A. Matthew 18:23-34

_____

_____

_____

B. Ezekiel 33:11

_____

_____

_____

C. Luke 15:11-32

_____

_____

_____

How is Jesus "merciful"?

A. John 8:1-11

_____

_____

_____

B. Mark 2:17

_____

_____

_____

C. Matthew 18:21-22

_____

_____

_____

D. Colossians 2:14

_____

_____

_____

E. Romans 8:1

_____

_____

_____

Return of the Prodigal Son, Rembrandt

What does this beatitude call us to do?

A. Colossians 3:12-13

_____

_____

_____

B. Matthew 6:9-15

_____

_____

_____

C. Ephesians 4:31-32

_____

_____

_____

Summary Statement

Who Are the Blessed?

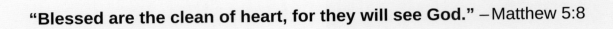

> **"Blessed are the clean of heart, for they will see God."** – Matthew 5:8

Who are the "clean of heart"?

A. 1 Samuel 16:7

_____

_____

_____

B. Matthew 23:27-28

_____

_____

_____

C. Matthew 5:28

_____

_____

_____

How is Jesus "clean of heart"?

A. Matthew 4:1-11

_____

_____

_____

B. Hebrews 7:26

_____

_____

_____

C. 2 Corinthians 5:21

_____

_____

_____

What does this beatitude call us to do?

A. Matthew 7:5

_____

_____

_____

B. Matthew 6:2-4

_____

_____

_____

C. Mark 7:14-15; 21-23

_____

_____

_____

D. Mark 1:15

_____

_____

_____

Resurrection of Christ, Bl. Fra Angelico

Summary Statement

Who Are the Blessed?

■

> **"Blessed are the peacemakers, for they will be called children of God."**
> —Matthew 5:9

Who are the "peacemakers"?

A. Matthew 7:12

_____

_____

_____

B. Ephesians 4:1-3

_____

_____

_____

C. James 3:18

_____

_____

_____

How is Jesus a "peacemaker"?

A. Ephesians 2:14

_____

_____

_____

B. Philippians 4:7

_____

_____

_____

C. John 20:21-22

_____

_____

_____

D. John 14:27

_____

_____

_____

E. Matthew 10:34-36

_____

_____

_____

The Holy Family, Juan Simón Gutiérrez

What does this beatitude call us to do?

A. Romans 12:18

_____

_____

_____

B. Philippians 4:6-7

_____

_____

_____

Summary Statement

Who Are the Blessed?

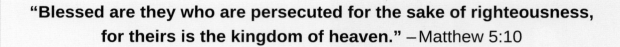

"Blessed are they who are persecuted for the sake of righteousness, for theirs is the kingdom of heaven." —Matthew 5:10

Who are the "persecuted"?

A. John 15:18-20

_____

_____

_____

B. 1 Corinthians 4:12-13

_____

_____

_____

How is Jesus "persecuted"?

A. Matthew 20:18-19

_____

_____

_____

B. Mark 15:15-39

_____

_____

_____

What does this beatitude call us to do?

A. Matthew 10:16-25

_____

_____

_____

B. 2 Corinthians 12:10

_____

_____

_____

C. Luke 9:23-24

_____

_____

_____

Summary Statement

The Beatitudes Prayer

Directions: Write your assigned beatitude in the space on the left. Using the prompts on the right, compose your prayer, including statements of thanksgiving and petition.

Beatitude	Petitions
	Thanksgiving Lord, we thank you for ... **Asking/Petition** We ask, Lord ... **We pray to the Lord ... Lord, hear our prayer.**

Answer Key

Sacred Art and the Beatitudes: Who Are the Blessed?

1. Accept reasoned answers.

2. Accept reasoned answers.

3. He descended into Hell.

4. The two figures are Adam and Eve.

5. He is strong, determined, firm, bold, undaunted, triumphant.

6. Jesus' Church defeats hell. If we believe in Him and keep his Commandments, we will never be separated from God.. The battle is already won; Jesus has won it for us.

Background Essay: Who Are the Blessed?

1. Because that message was the key to His teaching and He wanted everyone to hear it.

2. The modern definition focuses on pleasure. The classical definition involves being satisfied in our desire to be satisfied.

3. Imperfect happiness is the temporary pleasure that comes from earthly goods. Perfect happiness comes when we behold the beatific vision of God, who is all good. Jesus is teaching about perfect happiness.

4. Accept reasoned answers.

Handout A

> ### "Blessed are the poor in spirit, for theirs is the kingdom of Heaven."
> —Matthew 5:3

Who are the "poor in spirit"?

A. James 2:5 – Listen, my beloved brothers. Did God not choose those who are poor in the world to be rich in faith and heirs of the kingdom that he promised to those who love him?

B. 2 Corinthians 6:10 – as sorrowful yet always rejoicing; as poor yet enriching many; as having nothing and yet possessing all things.

How is Jesus "poor"?

A. 2 Corinthians 8:9 – For you know the gracious act of our Lord Jesus Christ, that for your sake he became poor although he was rich, so that by his poverty you might become rich.

B. Three Kinds of Poverty

1. Material Poverty

   a. Luke 2:7 – and she gave birth to her firstborn son. She wrapped him in swaddling clothes and laid him in a manger, because there was no room for them in the inn.

b. Luke 2:22-24 – When the days were completed for their purification according to the law of Moses, they took him up to Jerusalem to present him to the Lord, just as it is written in the law of the Lord, "Every male that opens the womb shall be consecrated to the Lord," and to offer the sacrifice of "a pair of turtledoves or two young pigeons," in accordance with the dictate in the law of the Lord.

c. Leviticus 12:8 – If, however, she cannot afford a lamb, she may take two turtledoves or two pigeons, the one for a holocaust and the other for a sin offering. The priest shall make atonement for her, and thus she will again be clean.

2. Poverty of Family and Friends

a. Matthew 10:37 – Whoever loves father or mother more than me is not worthy of me, and whoever loves son or daughter more than me is not worthy of me.

b. Matthew 12:46-50 – While he was still speaking to the crowds, his mother and his brothers appeared outside, wishing to speak with him. [Someone told him, "Your mother and your brothers are standing outside, asking to speak with you."] But he said in reply to the one who told him, "Who is my mother? Who are my brothers?" And stretching out his hand toward his disciples, he said, "Here are my mother and my brothers. For whoever does the will of my heavenly Father is my brother, and sister, and mother.

c. Luke 23:44-49 – When all the people who had gathered for this spectacle saw what had happened, they returned home beating their breasts; but all his acquaintances stood at a distance, including the women who had followed him from Galilee and saw these events.

3. Poverty of earthly power and glory

a. John 18:33-37 – Jesus answered, "My kingdom does not belong to this world. If my kingdom did belong to this world, my attendants [would] be fighting to keep me from being handed over to the Jews. But as it is, my kingdom is not here."

b. Matthew 4:8-10 – Then the devil took him up to a very high mountain, and showed him all the kingdoms of the world in their magnificence, and he said to him, "All these I shall give to you, if you will prostrate yourself and worship me." At this, Jesus said to him, "Get away, Satan! It is written: The Lord, your God, shall you worship and him alone shall you serve."

c. Philippians 2:6-7 – Who, though he was in the form of God, did not regard equality with God something to be grasped. Rather, he emptied himself, taking the form of a slave, coming in human likeness; and found human in appearance, he humbled himself, becoming obedient to death, even death on a cross.

What does this beatitude call us to do?

A. Matthew 19:16-22 – Now someone approached him and said, "Teacher, what good must I do to gain eternal life?" He answered him, "Why do you ask me about the good? There is only One who is good. If you wish to enter into life, keep the commandments." He asked him, "Which ones?" And Jesus replied, " 'You shall not kill; you shall not commit adultery; you shall not steal; you shall not bear false witness; honor your father and your mother'; and 'you shall love your neighbor as yourself.' "
The young man said to him, "All of these I have observed. What do I still lack?" Jesus said to him, "If you wish to be perfect, go, sell what you have and give to [the] poor, and you will have treasure in heaven. Then come, follow me." When the young man heard this statement, he went away sad, for he had many possessions. Then Jesus said to his disciples, "Amen, I say to you, it will be hard for one who is rich to enter the kingdom of heaven. Again I say to you, it is easier for a camel to pass through the eye of a needle than for one who is rich to enter the kingdom of God."

B. Matthew 18:8-9 – If your hand or foot causes you to sin, cut it off and throw it away. It is better for you to enter into life maimed or crippled than with two hands or two feet to be thrown into eternal fire. And if your eye causes you to sin, tear it out and throw it away. It is better for you to enter into life with one eye than with two eyes to be thrown into fiery Gehenna.

Summary Statement

The poor in spirit are those who share in the poverty of Christ, who, although He had nothing on Earth, possessed everything in Heaven. Jesus experienced three kinds of poverty during his earthly life; material poverty, poverty of friends and family, and poverty of earthly power and glory. We are called to be poor in spirit by actively seeking to remove from our lives all things that prevent us from having a true relationship with Jesus Christ and attaining heaven. For some, like the rich young man of the Gospel, that may be material wealth, but for others it may be pride, or another spiritual obstacle.

Handout B

> **"Blessed are they who mourn [now weeping],**
> **for they will be comforted."** —Matthew 5:4

Who are those who "mourn" or "weep"?

A. Romans 8:19-23 – For creation awaits with eager expectation the revelation of the children of God; for creation was made subject to futility, not of its own accord but because of the one who subjected it, in hope that creation itself would be set free from slavery to corruption and share in the glorious freedom of the children of God. We know that all creation is groaning in labor pains even until now; and not only that, but we ourselves, who have the first fruits of the Spirit, we also groan within ourselves as we wait for adoption, the redemption of our bodies.

B. Matthew 26:74-75 – At that he began to curse and to swear, "I do not know the man." And immediately a cock crowed. Then Peter remembered the word that Jesus had spoken: "Before the cock crows you will deny me three times." He went out and began to weep bitterly.

C. Romans 12:15 – Rejoice with those who rejoice, weep with those who weep.

D. Psalm 137:1-4 – By the rivers of Babylon there we sat weeping when we remembered Zion. On the poplars in its midst we hung up our harps. For there our captors asked us for the words of a song; Our tormentors, for joy: "Sing for us a song of Zion!" But how could we sing a song of the LORD in a foreign land?

E. Psalm 42:3, 10 – My soul thirsts for God, the living God. When can I enter and see the face of God?
I will say to God, my rock:
"Why do you forget me? Why must I go about mourning with the enemy oppressing me?"

How does Jesus "mourn" or "weep"?

A. Hebrews 12:2 – For the sake of the joy that lay before him he endured the cross, despising its shame, and has taken his seat at the right of the throne of God.

B. John 11:32-35 – When Mary came to where Jesus was and saw him, she fell at his feet and said to him, "Lord, if you had been here, my brother would not have died." When Jesus saw her weeping and the Jews who had come with her weeping, he became perturbed and deeply troubled, and said, "Where have you laid him?" They said to him, "Sir, come and see." And Jesus wept.

What does this beatitude call us to do?

A. Hebrews 12:1-3 – Therefore, since we are surrounded by so great a cloud of witnesses, let us rid ourselves of every burden and sin that clings to us and persevere in running the race that lies before us while keeping our eyes fixed on Jesus, the leader and perfecter of faith. For the sake of the joy that lay before him he endured the cross, despising its shame, and has taken his seat at the right of the throne of God. Consider how he endured such opposition from sinners, in order that you may not grow weary and lose heart.

B. 1 Peter 4:12-14 – Beloved, do not be surprised that a trial by fire is occurring among you, as if something strange were happening to you. But rejoice to the extent that you share in the sufferings of Christ, so that when his glory is revealed you may also rejoice exultantly. If you are insulted for the name of Christ, blessed are you, for the Spirit of glory and of God rests upon you.

C. Psalm 71:23 – My lips will shout for joy as I sing your praise; my soul, too, which you have redeemed.

D. 1 Peter 3:15 – Always be ready to give an explanation to anyone who asks you for a reason for your hope.

Summary Statement

The Bible speaks of many reasons to mourn or to weep; we mourn and weep in anticipation of our salvation, we mourn in sorrow for our sins, we mourn with others, and weep when we are alone or exiled or feel far from God. Jesus Himself mourned and wept, specifically to bring us our salvation from the eternal punishment of death. In light of this beatitude, we are called to persevere for the sake of the joy of the Good News of salvation and the coming of Christ. We should praise God in all things, even in our suffering, and always be prepared to explain the reason for our hope.

Handout C

"Blessed are the meek, for they will inherit the land." – Matthew 5:5

Who are "meek"?

A. Mark 9:35 – Then he sat down, called the Twelve, and said to them, "If anyone wishes to be first, he shall be the last of all and the servant of all.

B. Proverbs 15:1 – A mild answer turns back wrath, but a harsh word stirs up anger.

C. Proverbs 15:4 – A soothing tongue is a tree of life, but a perverse one breaks the spirit.

D. Sirach 6:5 – Pleasant speech multiplies friends, and gracious lips, friendly greetings.

How is Jesus "meek"?

A. Matthew 11:29 – Take my yoke upon you and learn from me, for I am meek and humble of heart; and you will find rest for yourselves.

B. John 13:1-17 – Before the feast of Passover, Jesus knew that his hour had come to pass from this world to the Father. He loved his own in the world and he loved them to the end. The devil had already induced Judas, son of Simon the Iscariot, to hand him over. So, during supper, fully aware that the Father had put everything into his power and that he had come from God and was returning to God, he rose from supper and took off his outer garments. He took a towel and tied it around his waist. Then he poured water into a basin and began to wash the disciples' feet and dry them with the towel around his waist. He came to Simon Peter, who said to him, "Master, are you going to wash my feet?" Jesus answered and said to him, "What I am doing, you do not understand now, but you will understand later." Peter said to him, "You will never wash my feet." Jesus answered him, "Unless I wash you, you will have no inheritance with me." Simon Peter said to him, "Master, then not only my feet, but my hands and head as well." Jesus said to him, "Whoever has bathed has no need except to have his feet washed, for he is clean all over; so you are clean, but not all." For he knew who would betray him; for this reason, he said, "Not all of you are clean." So when he had washed their feet [and] put his garments back on and reclined at table again, he said to them, "Do you realize what I have done for you? You call me 'teacher' and 'master,' and rightly so, for indeed I am. If I, therefore, the master and teacher, have washed your feet, you ought to wash one another's feet. I have given you a model to follow, so that as I have done for you, you should also do. Amen, amen, I say to you, no slave is greater than his master nor any messenger greater than the one who sent him. If you understand this, blessed are you if you do it.

C. 1 Peter 2:23 – When he was insulted, he returned no insult; when he suffered, he did not threaten; instead, he handed himself over to the one who judges justly.

D. Matthew 21:1-9 – When they drew near Jerusalem and came to Bethphage on the Mount of Olives, Jesus sent two disciples, saying to them, "Go into the village opposite you, and immediately you will find an ass tethered, and a colt with her. Untie them and bring them here to me. And if anyone should say anything to you, reply, 'The master has need of them.' Then he will send them at once." This happened so that what had been spoken through the prophet might be fulfilled: "Say to daughter Zion, 'Behold, your king comes to you, meek and riding on an ass, and on a colt, the foal of a beast of burden.' "

What does this beatitude call us to do?

A. 1 Peter 3:15 – But sanctify Christ as Lord in your hearts. Always be ready to give an explanation to anyone who asks you for a reason for your hope

B. Matthew 16:24 – Then Jesus said to his disciples, "Whoever wishes to come after me must deny himself, take up his cross, and follow me."

C. Galatians 5:22-26 – In contrast, the fruit of the Spirit is love, joy, peace, patience, kindness, generosity, faithfulness, gentleness, self-control. Against such there is no law. Now those who belong to Christ [Jesus] have crucified their flesh with its passions and desires. If we live in the Spirit, let us also follow the Spirit. Let us not be conceited, provoking one another, envious of one another.

D. 1 Colossians 3:12 – Put on then, as God's chosen ones, holy and beloved, heartfelt compassion, kindness, humility, gentleness, and patience.

Summary Statement

The meek are characterized not as shy or withdrawn, but as those who serve others in a spirit of unity, mildness, and kindness of speech. Jesus exemplified this kind of meekness and humility, claiming that his path gives peace. He modeled how to serve others by washing the disciples' feet, embracing his own suffering and death, and rejecting earthly power and glory. We are called to follow in Christ's footsteps and be ready to give a reason for our hope, carrying our own crosses in our lives, and building unity with each other in the Holy Spirit.

Handout D

> ## "Blessed are they who hunger and thirst for righteousness, for they will be satisfied." —Matthew 5:6

Who are the "hungry and thirsty"?

A. Luke 1:53 – Put on then, as God's chosen ones, holy and beloved, heartfelt compassion, kindness, humility, gentleness, and patience.

B. Luke 6:25 – But woe to you who are filled now, for you will be hungry. Woe to you who laugh now, for you will grieve and weep.

C. Luke 12:34 – For where your treasure is, there also will your heart be.

How does Jesus "satisfy"?

A. John 6:35, 53-58 – Jesus said to them, "I am the bread of life; whoever comes to me will never hunger, and whoever believes in me will never thirst." Jesus said to them, "Amen, amen, I say to you, unless you eat the flesh of the Son of Man and drink his blood, you do not have life within you. Whoever eats my flesh and drinks my blood has eternal life, and I will raise him on the last day. For my flesh is true food, and my blood is true drink. Whoever eats my flesh and drinks my blood remains in me and I in him. Just as the living Father sent me and I have life because of the Father, so also the one who feeds on me will have life because of me. This is the bread that came down from heaven. Unlike your ancestors who ate and still died, whoever eats this bread will live forever."

B. John 4:13-15 – Jesus answered and said to her, "Everyone who drinks this water will be thirsty again; but whoever drinks the water I shall give will never thirst; the water I shall give will become in him a spring of water welling up to eternal life." The woman said to him, "Sir, give me this water, so that I may not be thirsty or have to keep coming here to draw water."

C. 1 Peter 2:21 – For to this you have been called, because Christ also suffered for you, leaving you an example that you should follow in his footsteps.

What does this beatitude call us to do?

A. Matthew 22:37-40 – He said to him, "You shall love the Lord, your God, with all your heart, with all your soul, and with all your mind. This is the greatest and the first commandment. The second is like it: You shall love your neighbor as yourself. The whole law and the prophets depend on these two commandments."

B. Matthew 25:31-46 – When the Son of Man comes in his glory, and all the angels with him, he will sit upon his glorious throne, and all the nations will be assembled before him. And he will separate them one from another, as a shepherd separates the sheep from the goats. He will place the sheep on his right and the goats on his left. Then the king will say to those on his right, "Come, you who are blessed by my Father. Inherit the kingdom prepared for you from the foundation of the world. For I was hungry and you gave me food, I was thirsty and you gave me drink, a stranger and you welcomed me, naked and you clothed me, ill and you cared for me, in prison and you visited me." Then the righteous will answer him and say, "Lord, when did we see you hungry and feed you, or thirsty and give you drink? When did we see you a stranger and welcome you, or naked and clothe you? When did we see you ill or in prison, and visit you?" And the king will say to them in reply, "Amen, I say to you, whatever you did for one of these least brothers of mine, you did for me." Then he will say to those on his left, "Depart from me, you accursed, into the eternal fire prepared for the devil and his angels. For I was hungry and you gave me no food, I was thirsty and you gave me no drink, stranger and you gave me no welcome, naked and you gave me no clothing, ill and in prison, and you did not care for me." Then they will answer and say, "Lord, when did we see you hungry or thirsty or a stranger or naked or ill or in prison, and not minister to your needs?" He will answer them, "Amen, I say to you, what you did not do for one of these least ones, you did not do for me." And these will go off to eternal punishment, but the righteous to eternal life.

Summary Statement

Jesus' teaching directs us to hunger for or desire things in right order, specifically, that which is righteous, or of God. Scripture tells us that the righteous are compassionate, kind, humble, gentle, and patient. Those who desire or hunger for worldly things, will not find satisfaction. Jesus taught that He is true bread and true drink, which we encounter in the Eucharist, and that only He will satisfy infinitely. We are then called to be righteous in our own lives, that is, to love God above all things, and to love our neighbors as ourselves. This is lived by following the law of God and by serving others.

Handout E

> ## "Blessed are the merciful, for they will be shown mercy." —Matthew 5:7

Who are the "merciful"?

A. Matthew 18:23-34 – That is why the kingdom of heaven may be likened to a king who decided to settle accounts with his servants. When he began the accounting, a debtor was brought before him who owed him a huge amount. Since he had no way of paying it back, his master ordered him to be sold, along with his wife, his children, and all his property, in payment of the debt. At that, the servant fell down, did him homage, and said, "Be patient with me, and I will pay you back in full." Moved with compassion the master of that servant let him go and forgave him the loan. When that servant had left, he found one of his fellow servants who owed him a much smaller amount. He seized him and started to choke him, demanding, "Pay back what you owe." Falling to his knees, his fellow servant begged him, "Be patient with me, and I will pay you back." But he refused. Instead, he had him put in prison until he paid back the debt. Now when his fellow servants saw what had happened, they were deeply disturbed, and went to their master and reported the whole affair. His master summoned him and said to him, "You wicked servant! I forgave you your entire debt because you begged me to. Should you not have had pity on your fellow servant, as I had pity on you?" Then in anger his master handed him over to the torturers until he should pay back the whole debt.

B. Ezekiel 33:11 – Answer them: As I live—oracle of the Lord GOD—I swear I take no pleasure in the death of the wicked, but rather that they turn from their ways and live. Turn, turn from your evil ways! Why should you die, house of Israel?

C. Luke 15:11-32 – Then he said, "A man had two sons, and the younger son said to his father, 'Father, give me the share of your estate that should come to me.' So the father divided the property between them. After a few days, the younger son collected all his belongings and set off to a distant country where he squandered his inheritance on a life of dissipation. When he had freely spent everything, a severe famine struck that country, and he found himself in dire need. So he hired himself out to one of the local citizens who sent him to his farm to tend the swine. And he longed to eat his fill of the pods on which the swine fed, but nobody gave him any. Coming to his senses he thought, 'How many of my father's hired workers have more than enough food to eat, but here am I, dying from hunger. I shall get up and go to my father and I shall say to him, 'Father, I have sinned against heaven and against you. I no longer deserve to be called your son; treat me as you would treat one of your hired workers.' So he got up and went back to his father. While he was still a long way off, his father caught sight of him, and was filled with compassion. He ran to his son, embraced him and kissed him. His son said to him, 'Father, I have sinned against heaven and against you; I no longer deserve to be called your son.' But his father ordered his servants, 'Quickly bring the finest robe and put it on him; put a ring on his finger and sandals on his feet. Take the fattened calf and slaughter it. Then let us celebrate with a feast, because this son of mine was dead, and has come to life again; he was lost, and has been found.' Then the celebration began. Now the older son had been out in the field and, on his way back, as he neared the house, he heard the sound of music and dancing. He called one of the servants and asked what this might mean. The servant said to him, 'Your brother has returned and your father has slaughtered the fattened calf because he has him back safe and sound.' He became angry, and when he refused to enter the house, his father came out and pleaded with him. He said to his father in reply, 'Look, all these years I served you and not once did I disobey your orders; yet you never gave me even a young goat to feast on with my friends. But when your son returns who swallowed up your property with prostitutes, for him you slaughter the fattened calf.' He said to him, 'My son, you are here with me always; everything I have is yours. But now we must celebrate and rejoice, because your

brother was dead and has come to life again; he was lost and has been found.' "

How is Jesus "merciful"?

A. John 8:1-11 – Then each went to his own house while Jesus went to the Mount of Olives. But early in the morning he arrived again in the temple area, and all the people started coming to him, and he sat down and taught them. Then the scribes and the Pharisees brought a woman who had been caught in adultery and made her stand in the middle. They said to him, "Teacher, this woman was caught in the very act of committing adultery. Now in the law, Moses commanded us to stone such women. So what do you say?" They said this to test him, so that they could have some charge to bring against him. Jesus bent down and began to write on the ground with his finger. But when they continued asking him, he straightened up and said to them, "Let the one among you who is without sin be the first to throw a stone at her." Again he bent down and wrote on the ground. And in response, they went away one by one, beginning with the elders. So he was left alone with the woman before him. Then Jesus straightened up and said to her, "Woman, where are they? Has no one condemned you?" She replied, "No one, sir." Then Jesus said, "Neither do I condemn you. Go, [and] from now on do not sin any more."

B. Mark 2:17 – Jesus heard this and said to them [that], "Those who are well do not need a physician, but the sick do. I did not come to call the righteous but sinners."

C. Matthew 18:21-22 – Then Peter approaching asked him, "Lord, if my brother sins against me, how often must I forgive him? As many as seven times?" Jesus answered, "I say to you, not seven times but seventy-seven times."

D. Colossians 2:14 – Obliterating the bond against us, with its legal claims, which was opposed to us, he also removed it from our midst, nailing it to the cross.

E. Romans 8:1 – Hence, now there is no condemnation for those who are in Christ Jesus.

What does this beatitude call us to do?

A. Colossians 3:12-13 – Put on then, as God's chosen ones, holy and beloved, heartfelt compassion, kindness, humility, gentleness, and patience, bearing with one another and forgiving one another, if one has a grievance against another; as the Lord has forgiven you, so must you also do.

B. Matthew 6:9-15 – This is how you are to pray: Our Father in heaven, hallowed be your name, your kingdom come, your will be done, on earth as in heaven. Give us today our daily bread; and forgive us our debts, as we forgive our debtors; and do not subject us to the final test, but deliver us from the evil one. If you forgive others their transgressions, your heavenly Father will forgive you. But if you do not forgive others, neither will your Father forgive your transgressions.

C. Ephesians 4:31-32 – All bitterness, fury, anger, shouting, and reviling must be removed from you, along with all malice. [And] be kind to one another, compassionate, forgiving one another as God has forgiven you in Christ.

Summary Statement

The merciful are those who, unlike the servant of the parable, forgive others because God first forgave them. The merciful give what they have themselves received, mercy. The merciful forgive as the Father Himself forgives, which is unconditionally, and it is in this forgiveness that the merciful find their joy. Jesus Himself forgave the sins of many and did so without condemnation and as often as necessary, but always called the sinner to sin no more. Christ's death on the Cross brought forgiveness for our sinfulness and removed our deserved punishment. We are called to forgive as Christ forgave, to give the forgiveness that we ourselves have received so that we might be kind and compassionate toward one another.

Handout F

> **"Blessed are the clean of heart, for they will see God."** — Matthew 5:8

Who are the "clean of heart"?

A. 1 Samuel 16:7 — But the LORD said to Samuel: Do not judge from his appearance or from his lofty stature, because I have rejected him. God does not see as a mortal, who sees the appearance. The LORD looks into the heart.

B. Matthew 23:27-28 — Woe to you, scribes and Pharisees, you hypocrites. You are like whitewashed tombs, which appear beautiful on the outside, but inside are full of dead men's bones and every kind of filth. Even so, on the outside you appear righteous, but inside you are filled with hypocrisy and evildoing.

C. Matthew 5:28 — But I say to you, everyone who looks at a woman with lust has already committed adultery with her in his heart.

How is Jesus "clean of heart"?

A. Matthew 4:1-11 — Then Jesus was led by the Spirit into the desert to be tempted by the devil. He fasted for forty days and forty nights, and afterwards he was hungry. The tempter approached and said to him, "If you are the Son of God, command that these stones become loaves of bread." He said in reply, "It is written: 'One does not live by bread alone, but by every word that comes forth from the mouth of God.'" Then the devil took him to the holy city, and made him stand on the parapet of the temple, and said to him, "If you are the Son of God, throw yourself down. For it is written: 'He will command his angels concerning you' and 'with their hands they will support you, lest you dash your foot against a stone.'" Jesus answered him, "Again it is written, 'You shall not put the Lord, your God, to the test.'" Then the devil took him up to a very high mountain, and showed him all the kingdoms of the world in their magnificence, and he said to him, "All these I shall give to you, if you will prostrate yourself and worship me." At this, Jesus said to him, "Get away, Satan! It is written: 'The Lord, your God, shall you worship and him alone shall you serve.'" Then the devil left him and, behold, angels came and ministered to him.

B. Hebrews 7:26 – It was fitting we should have such a high priest: holy, innocent, undefiled, separated from sinners, higher than the heavens.

C. 2 Corinthians 5:21 – For our sake he made him to be sin who did not know sin, so that we might become the righteousness of God in him.

What does this Beatitude call us to do?

A. Matthew 7:5 – You hypocrite, remove the wooden beam from your eye first; then you will see clearly to remove the splinter from your brother's eye.

B. Matthew 6:2-4 – When you give alms, do not blow a trumpet before you, as the hypocrites do in the synagogues and in the streets to win the praise of others. Amen, I say to you, they have received their reward. But when you give alms, do not let your left hand know what your right is doing, so that your almsgiving may be secret. And your Father who sees in secret will repay you.

C. Mark 7:14-15; 21-23 – He summoned the crowd again and said to them, "Hear me, all of you, and understand. Nothing that enters one from outside can defile that person; but the things that come out from within are what defile."
"From within people, from their hearts, come evil thoughts, unchastity, theft, murder, adultery, greed, malice, deceit, licentiousness, envy, blasphemy, arrogance, folly. All these evils come from within and they defile."

D. Mark 1:15 – This is the time of fulfillment. The kingdom of God is at hand. Repent, and believe in the gospel.

Summary Statement

The clean or pure-hearted are those whose actions on the outside match who they are on the inside. This includes chastity, as this beatitude is popularly understood to be referring to, but means more than that. Jesus compared the clean of heart to the opposite of the hypocritical Pharisees of His time who went through the outward motions of keeping the Law, but were empty in their hearts. Jesus was clean of heart because He was free of sin and resisted all human temptation for worldly desire and earthly power. He who was innocent of sin took on our sins so that we could be purified. We are called to repent of our sins and believe in the Good News of our salvation. We must strive to make sure that our actions and piety truly come from the heart and truly transform our hearts and we must avoid the temptations and sin that defile us and make us unclean, without judging our neighbor.

Handout G

> **"Blessed are the peacemakers, for they will be called children of God."**
> — Matthew 5:9

Who are the "peacemakers"?

A. Matthew 7:12 – Do to others whatever you would have them do to you. This is the law and the prophets.

B. Ephesians 4:1-3 – I, then, a prisoner for the Lord, urge you to live in a manner worthy of the call you have received, with all humility and gentleness, with patience, bearing with one another through love, striving to preserve the unity of the spirit through the bond of peace.

C. James 3:18 – And the fruit of righteousness is sown in peace for those who cultivate peace.

How is Jesus a "peacemaker"?

A. Ephesians 2:14 – For he is our peace, he who made both one and broke down the dividing wall of enmity, through his flesh.

B. Philippians 4:7 – Then the peace of God that surpasses all understanding will guard your hearts and minds in Christ Jesus.

C. John 20:21-22 – [Jesus] said to them again, "Peace be with you. As the Father has sent me, so I send you." And when he had said this, he breathed on them and said to them, "Receive the holy Spirit."

D. John 14:27 – Peace I leave with you; my peace I give to you. Not as the world gives do I give it to you. Do not let your hearts be troubled or afraid.

E. Matthew 10:34-36 – Do not think that I have come to bring peace upon the earth. I have come to bring not peace but the sword. For I have come to set a man "against his father, a daughter against her mother, and a daughter-in-law against her mother-in-law; and one's enemies will be those of his household."

What does this beatitude call us to do?

A. Romans 12:18 — If possible, on your part, live at peace with all.

B. Philippians 4:6-7 — Have no anxiety at all, but in everything, by prayer and petition, with thanksgiving, make your requests known to God. Then the peace of God that surpasses all understanding will guard your hearts and minds in Christ Jesus.

Summary Statement

The peacemaker is one who treats others the way he or she would want to be treated, that is, with humility, gentleness, patience, and common support through love, in the unity of the Holy Spirit. Those who make peace are righteous in God's eyes. Jesus is our peace and He gives us His peace, through the Holy Spirit, by which we are sent to proclaim His peace to the world. The peace of Christ, however, is not accepted by all, and may cause division when unaccepted or rejected. We are called to live in peace with everyone, through prayer and thanksgiving, and above all, by placing our trust in Jesus.

Handout H

> **"Blessed are they who are persecuted for the sake of righteousness, for theirs is the kingdom of heaven."** —Matthew 5:10

Who are the "persecuted"?

A. John 15: 18-20 – If the world hates you, realize that it hated me first. If you belonged to the world, the world would love its own; but because you do not belong to the world, and I have chosen you out of the world, the world hates you. Remember the word I spoke to you, "No slave is greater than his master." If they persecuted me, they will also persecute you. If they kept my word, they will also keep yours.

B. 1 Corinthians 4:12-13 – And we toil, working with our own hands. When ridiculed, we bless; when persecuted, we endure; when slandered, we respond gently. We have become like the world's rubbish, the scum of all, to this very moment.

How is Jesus "persecuted"?

A. Matthew 20:18-19 – Behold, we are going up to Jerusalem, and the Son of Man will be handed over to the chief priests and the scribes, and they will condemn him to death, and hand him over to the Gentiles to be mocked and scourged and crucified, and he will be raised on the third day.

B. Mark 15:15-39 – So Pilate, wishing to satisfy the crowd, released Barabbas to them and, after he had Jesus scourged, handed him over to be crucified. The soldiers led him away inside the palace, that is, the praetorium, and assembled the whole cohort. They clothed him in purple and, weaving a crown of thorns, placed it on him. They began to salute him with, "Hail, King of the Jews!" and kept striking his head with a reed and spitting upon him. They knelt before him in homage. And when they had mocked him, they stripped him of the purple cloak, dressed him in his own clothes, and led him out to crucify him. They pressed into service a passer-by, Simon, a Cyrenian, who was coming in from the country, the father of Alexander and Rufus, to carry his cross. They brought him to the place of Golgotha (which is translated Place of the Skull). They gave him wine drugged with myrrh, but he did not take it. Then they crucified him and divided his garments by casting lots for them to see what each should take. It was nine o'clock in the morning when they crucified him. The inscription of the charge against him read, "The King of the Jews." With him they crucified two revolutionaries, one on his right and one on his left. Those passing by reviled him, shaking their heads and saying, "Aha! You who would destroy the temple and rebuild it in three days, save yourself by coming down from the cross." Likewise the chief priests, with the scribes, mocked him among themselves and said, "He saved others; he cannot save himself. Let the Messiah, the King of Israel, come down now from the cross that we may see and believe." Those who were

crucified with him also kept abusing him.
The Death of Jesus. At noon darkness came over the whole land until three in the afternoon. And at three o'clock Jesus cried out in a loud voice, "*Eloi, Eloi, lema sabachthani?*" which is translated, "My God, my God, why have you forsaken me?" Some of the bystanders who heard it said, "Look, he is calling Elijah." One of them ran, soaked a sponge with wine, put it on a reed, and gave it to him to drink, saying, "Wait, let us see if Elijah comes to take him down." Jesus gave a loud cry and breathed his last. The veil of the sanctuary was torn in two from top to bottom. When the centurion who stood facing him saw how he breathed his last he said, "Truly this man was the Son of God!"

What does this beatitude call us to do?

A. Matthew 10:16-25 – Behold, I am sending you like sheep in the midst of wolves; so be shrewd as serpents and simple as doves. But beware of people, for they will hand you over to courts and scourge you in their synagogues, and you will be led before governors and kings for my sake as a witness before them and the pagans. When they hand you over, do not worry about how you are to speak or what you are to say. You will be given at that moment what you are to say. For it will not be you who speak but the Spirit of your Father speaking through you. Brother will hand over brother to death, and the father his child; children will rise up against parents and have them put to death. You will be hated by all because of my name, but whoever endures to the end will be saved. When they persecute you in one town, flee to another. Amen, I say to you, you will not finish the towns of Israel before the Son of Man comes. No disciple is above his teacher, no slave above his master. It is enough for the disciple that he become like his teacher, for the slave that he become like his master. If they have called the master of the house Beelzebul, how much more those of his household!

B. 2 Corinthians 12:10 – Therefore, I am content with weaknesses, insults, hardships, persecutions, and constraints, for the sake of Christ; for when I am weak, then I am strong.

C. Luke 9:23-24 – Then he said to all, "If anyone wishes to come after me, he must deny himself and take up his cross daily and follow me. For whoever wishes to save his life will lose it, but whoever loses his life for my sake will save it.

Summary Statement

All those who follow in Christ's footsteps will be persecuted, because of the contrary message of the Gospel to society, who first persecuted Christ Himself. The persecuted, however, respond with blessings, gentleness and endurance. Jesus foretold of his own persecution and that He would overcome it. In Christ's Suffering, Passion, and Death on the Cross, He endured the greatest of persecution for our sake and so for the sake of the Kingdom of God. As witnesses of Christ, we are called to be like Christ, even unto death, and to endure our own crosses for His sake. In our weaknesses, we must rely on the strength of Christ.

Teacher Notes

The Beatitudes and the Saints

Overview

All the souls in heaven were once people on earth: sons, daughters, priests, religious, husbands, wives, friends. The saints give ample examples of just how rich and varied the call to holiness looks among the members of the Church. In this lesson, students assume the persona of a saint, and engage in discussions with classmates/other saints. Saint biography cards are provided here at two reading levels. With younger students, read the stories of 3 or 4 saints aloud and assign everyone in the class to play one of those four. Older students can do their own research to learn more about these individuals, and/or write new biography cards for saints not included in this guide.

Connection to the Catechism

→ CCC 2683

Essential Questions

→ What can the saints teach us about what it means to live a holy life?

→ How can I live my own vocation to beatitude?

Grade Levels

■ ES ■ MS ■ HS

Time

One fifty-minute class

BIBLICAL TOUCHSTONES

And I have given them the glory you gave me, so that they may be one, as we are one.

JOHN 17:22

Remember your leaders who spoke the word of God to you. Consider the outcome of their way of life and imitate their faith.

HEBREWS 13:7

Religious Icons Collection

Sacred Art and the Beatitudes
The Beatitudes and the Saints

 Religious Icons Collection

Directions: This image is a photograph of many religious icons. Take a few minutes to look at each individual icon as well as the photograph of all of them as a whole.

Conversation Questions

1. Have you ever seen paintings like the ones in this photograph? Where?

2. What is an icon?

3. How do these icons differ from art you see today on things like movie posters, print advertisements, billboards, and other places?

4. Catholics do not believe that Jesus or the saints are present in sculptures or icons, and we do not worship sculptures or icons. What are they used for?

5. What are some reasons Christians would have icons in their homes?

6. We are all called to be saints. What are some ways this collage of icons shows us that truth?

7. Many saints are pictured in icons with objects or symbols. If someone were to paint an icon of you, what objects or symbols might be included?

Lesson Plan

Student Materials

- Saint Cards
- Handout A: Saintly Dinner Party
- Handout B: Three Saint Stories

Background/Homework

If you make the saint assignments a few days ahead of time, students could be asked to bring in food from their saint's region and time period for the "dinner."

Warm-Up   *20 minutes*

A. Copy, cut out, and laminate sets of Saint Cards. Make each set on a different color paper.

B. Make enough sets so that every student in your class can receive one card. Have students familiarize themselves with the information on their card, and prepare to "become" that saint for next class. Variation: For younger students, select 3 or 4 saints and read their stories aloud. Then distribute cards for just those saints among students. Older students could be given cards as the basis for a longer biography or creative writing assignment.

C. Now encourage students to stand up and "mingle" as though at a dinner party with the other saints. (Keep students within color groups so they avoid "meeting" the same saint they are playing.) In their persona, they should introduce themselves; share a little bit about their lives, and so forth.

Activity   *20 minutes*

A. Have students now settle into groups of 4-8 for "dinner." If you had students bring in food for their saint, have them serve it now.

B. As students share a meal together, they should discuss some of the following questions. Write them on the board:

- Who are you and where are you from? When did you live?

- What gifts and talents did God bless you with, and how did you use them to serve God and your neighbor?

- What was your biggest challenge?

- What can people learn from your life?

Additional ideas:

- Sophisticated students could create and add new cards into the mix for individuals such as Cain, King Herod, Judas, Pontius Pilate, or others, and plan discussion questions that would bring to light differences in morality and discussions of good vs. evil.

- Prepare a Saint Card for yourself ahead of time, and act as a "surprise visitor" for dinner.

- Have all the St. Monicas come to the front of the room (or all the St. Pauls, all the St. Peters, etc.). Give the audience of students a chance to ask questions, and allow the students up front to confer on their answers.

- Have students write skits that tell the stories of their saints.

- Have "fishbowl" conversations between unexpected pairings of saints. For example, put St. Stephen with Bl. Miguel Pro. What topics of conversation arise?

Wrap-Up
10 minutes

Still in their dinner groups, have students begin **Handout A: Saintly Dinner Party** and finish it for homework.

Extension Options

A. Have students read **Handout B: Three Saint Stories** and complete the chart that follows.

B. Have students learn about the miracles attributed to their saint's intercession. They should report on what they find in a brief oral presentation.

C. Have students use their Bibles to look up the Scripture references that formed the basis of the Saint Cards for Sts. Paul, Peter, and Stephen. Have them draw a picture for each reference, or create a comic strip-type panel on poster board. A list is below:

St. Paul

Acts 9:1-20 – Paul's conversion

Acts 16:22-33 – Paul imprisoned and the earthquake

Acts 21 – Paul preaching in Jerusalem and accused

Acts 25:10-12 – Paul appeals to Caesar

Acts 27 – Paul's voyage and shipwreck

Acts 28 – Paul preaches in Rome

Paul's Letters: Romans, 1 Corinthians, 2 Corinthians, Galatians, Ephesians, Philippians, Colossians, 1 Thessalonians, 2 Thessalonians, 1 Timothy, 2 Timothy, Titus, and Philemon.

St. Peter

John 1:39-42 – Andrew introduces Peter and Jesus calls him

Matthew 16:13-18 – "You are Peter"

Matthew 17:1-8 – Transfiguration

Matthew 26:36-45 – Agony in the Garden

John 8:10-11 – Peter cuts off slave's ear

Matthew 26:31-35 – Jesus predicts Peter's denial

Luke 22:54-62 – Peter denies Jesus

John 21:15-17 – "Feed my Sheep"

Acts 1 – Peter speaks on Pentecost

Acts 3:1-8 – Peter's first miracle

Acts 15 – Council of Jerusalem

Acts 12:1-11 – Angel frees Peter

1 and 2 Peter – Peter's 2 Letters

St. Stephen

Acts 6 and 7

Bulletin Board Option

On large, different colored strips of paper, write out each of the Beatitudes. Post them at regular intervals on the bulletin board. Then make copies of the Saint Cards, and challenge students to match up saints with particular beatitudes. (For example, for "Blessed are those who mourn," students might select St. Monica.) They should write at least 3 or 4 sentences explaining how that particular saint lived the beatitude they chose. Display the saint pictures and student paragraphs.

Saint Cards

St. Jeanne D'Arc

1412-1431

Feast Day:
May 30

Jeanne D'Arc was born in a French village to a Catholic family. Her father was a farmer. Her mother could not read or write, but she taught Jeanne how to pray and how to work hard. During this time, England and France were at war. England ruled over the northern part of France, including the place where French kings were coronated (received their crowns).

When Jeanne was 13 years old she began hearing the voices of saints. Soon she began having visions as well. The archangel Michael, St. Margaret, and St. Catherine appeared to her and told her to help the French king fight the English. The king sent her into battle, and Jeanne led her troops to victory. The French won several more battles. The king was finally able to receive his crown at Reims Cathedral, and Jeanne was there for the ceremony. The French were on their way to winning the war with Jeanne's help.

But not everyone was happy with the French victories. Some French people wanted England to win. In 1430, Joan was captured by some of those people. She was put in an iron cage with chains on her neck, hands, and feet. At her trial, her captors questioned Jeanne about her visions. They knew she was a simple peasant girl, and they tried to trick her into saying that she was practicing witchcraft. But she refused to say she had not seen and heard the saints. She told the judges: "I saw them with these very eyes, as well as I see you."

Throughout of her trial, the French king did nothing to help her. Jeanne was convicted of witchcraft and heresy and burned alive. She was 19 years old. Thirty years later, a Church court declared that her trial had been unfair, and she was declared innocent of all crimes.

St. Jeanne D'Arc

1412-1431

Feast Day:
May 30

Jeanne D'Arc was born in a small French village. When Jeanne was a teenager, angels and saints appeared to her. The angels and saints told Jeanne to help the king of France in the war against England.

Jeanne led her troops to victory. The French were on their way to winning the war with Jeanne's help.

Some French people were mad about this. Even though they were French, they wanted England to win. They arrested Jeanne and put her in jail. They threw her in an iron cage. They put chains on her neck, hands, and feet.

At her trial, they asked Jeanne tricky questions to try to confuse her. They tried to get Jeanne to say she was a witch, and that her visions of saints were bad.

Even though Jeanne had helped him, the French king did nothing to help her.

Jeanne was convicted of witchcraft and heresy (speaking against the Church) and burned alive. She was 19 years old.

Thirty years later, a Church court said that her trial had been unfair. Jeanne was declared innocent of all crimes.

St. Francis of Assisi

1181-1226

Feast Day:
October 4

Francis was born into a rich Italian family. He enjoyed his wealth with wild, popular parties. One night while camping on his way to join the Fourth Crusade, God told him in a dream to return home. He did, and he started forming habits of prayer. While praying in a chapel, Christ spoke to him from the crucifix, "Francis, repair my church." Francis obeyed literally, fixing the chapel's walls and roof. Then he literally obeyed Christ's commands throughout the Gospels: Francis gave what he had to poor people and he preached the Good News. Many men joined Francis, gave away their possessions, and lived in poverty. They begged when they needed food and gave to poorer people whatever they did not need. Francis and his followers preached in Italy, Tunis, Morocco, and Egypt.

Francis wrote a rule to set out how he wanted himself and his followers to live. Pope Innocent III approved it. After several revisions, Pope Honorius III also approved it. A woman named Clare joined Francis, and she started a group of women called the Poor Clares. These women supported the Franciscans by praying before the Eucharist.

During the Crusades, Francis tried to make peace with the Sultan who was fighting the Christians. The Sultan was impressed by Francis, but refused to convert. While praying one evening, Francis received the stigmata. He died several weeks later. Franciscans and Poor Clares continue to live according the rules of St. Francis and St. Clare.

St. Francis of Assisi

1181-1226

Feast Day:
October 4

Francis was born into a rich Italian family. He had an easy life and had lots of friends.

Francis decided to fight in the Crusades. He was on his way to join the fight when God told him in a dream to return home. He obeyed and went home. Another day he was praying in a chapel. Christ spoke to Francis from the crucifix. Jesus said, "Francis, repair my church." Francis again did exactly what Jesus said. He started fixing the chapel's walls and roof. Then he followed Christ's commands from the Bible, giving what he had to poor people and telling them about God's love.

Many men joined Francis. They also gave away their possessions. They begged when they needed food. They gave whatever they did not need to poorer people.

The Crusades continued. Francis tried to make peace with the Sultan who was fighting the Christians. The Sultan liked Francis, but the war continued.

While praying one evening, Francis received the stigmata (wounds like the ones Jesus received on the Cross). He died several weeks later. Religious men all over the world today continue to live according the rules of St. Francis. They are known as Franciscans.

St. Augustine of Hippo

354-430

Feast Day:
August 28

Augustine was born on the northern coast of Africa, in the country we now call Algeria. His mother, St. Monica, was Christian. His father worked for the Roman Empire and was a pagan, but he allowed Augustine's mother to teach the family's three children about following Jesus.

Augustine was very bright, and his parents worked hard to send him to the best schools. He read the most challenging authors of the day. He became a popular speaker and teacher. But even though Augustine was achieving success in the eyes of the world, he was living a wicked life. Over time, thanks to the influence of his mother and the Bishop of Milan, St. Ambrose, Augustine came to believe that God's grace could save even a terrible sinner like him. He was converted to Christianity. He became a priest and, later, the Bishop of Hippo.

Augustine became one of the most important Christian writers in history. In his book *Confessions*, we wrote about his conversion. He explained how all of us naturally yearn to be with God. Augustine also spent time correcting people who had wrong ideas about Christianity. He spoke about love, and said the Church should always show mercy to those who repent. He argued against those who thought humans could achieve moral perfection through their own free will alone. Augustine knew that we need God's grace to be saved. When the most important city in the world was destroyed by the Visigoths (a barbarian tribe), many people felt like it was the end of the world. But in his book *De Civitate Dei (City of God)*, Augustine assured people that no pagan city on Earth could compare to Christians' true home: Heaven. He wrote more than 300 sermons.

Augustine was 75 when another barbarian tribe, the Vandals, started to attack his hometown of Hippo. He died that summer. He is one of the most important Church Fathers, and a Doctor of the Church.

St. Augustine

354-430

Feast Day:
August 28

Augustine was born on the northern coast of Africa. His mother was St. Monica. She spent her life sharing Jesus with her family.

Augustine was very bright. His parents sent him to the best schools. He read great books. He became a popular speaker and teacher.

But Augustine was living a wicked life. His mother and the Bishop of Milan, St. Ambrose, kept trying to help Augustine see that God's mercy had no limits. Finally Augustine was converted to Christianity. He became a priest. Later he was made Bishop of Hippo.

Augustine became one of the most important Christian writers ever. He wrote about how all of us want to be with God. He wrote about love. He said the Church should always show mercy. He wrote about how we need God's grace.

During Augustine's life, the city of Rome was destroyed. Many people were scared. But Augustine helped people see that Christians' true home was Heaven.

Augustine died when he was 75. He wrote hundreds of sermons and many important books. He gave hope to countless people. He is a Doctor of the Church. This is a very special title that means his writings helped form Catholic doctrine.

St. Teresa of Ávila

1515-1582

Feast Day:
October 15

Teresa Sánchez de Cepeda y Ahumada was born in the Ávila region of Spain. When she was younger she was caught up in her social life. She wanted to love God, but felt like she did not deserve to be close to Him. Her father sent her to a convent to help her straighten out her life. But the convent turned out to be more like a hotel, with frequent visitors and socializing. Teresa prayed to be closer to Jesus, but felt like He wasn't answering her. After 18 years, she felt like giving up.

When she was 41, a priest encouraged her to turn back to prayer. But it was hard for her. She felt like her mind was too busy and distracted to be able to focus on Jesus. But soon she felt very close to God. Praying became such an intense experience that she would cry. She would feel pain, and all her senses would be overwhelmed. Sometimes her whole body would even levitate (be raised up from the ground). These experiences scared Teresa and she especially disliked when they happened in public. But she knew Jesus was with her when He came to her in visions. Then she felt peaceful and encouraged.

Two years later she decided to start a new convent focused on prayer and living simply. Her reforms made a lot of people angry, but new Discalced Carmelite communities eventually spread throughout Europe. She wrote books about her life and her visions, even though many people said women shouldn't do those things. In 1970, Pope Paul VI named her a Doctor of the Church. This is a very special title that means her writings helped form Catholic doctrine.

St. Teresa of Ávila ■

1515–1582

Feast Day:
October 15

Teresa was born in a part of Spain called Ávila. When she was younger, she enjoyed being with friends and having fun. She wanted to love Jesus, but she worried she wasn't good enough.

Teresa's father sent her to a convent (a place where nuns live). But the convent was a bad place. The sisters there did not take their religious vows seriously.

Teresa prayed for almost 20 years. She felt like Jesus wasn't answering her. She almost gave up. But a priest encouraged her to keep trying. Then she finally started to feel like God was listening. When she prayed, she would start to cry. She would feel like she couldn't hear, see, smell, or even touch anything. Sometimes her body would even levitate (rise up off the ground). She didn't like it when these things happened to her where people could see.

But a lot of people were interested in what she had learned from God about praying. She wrote books about what she had learned. Teresa decided to start a new convent. Her convent would be focused on prayer and living simply. A lot of young ladies joined.

Long after she died, Pope Paul VI named her a Doctor of the Church. This is a very special title that means her writings helped form Catholic doctrine.

Bl. Chiara Luce Badano

1971–1990

Feast Day:
October 29

Chiara was born in a small Italian village to Catholic parents who had prayed for 11 years for a child. In kindergarten, she started saving her money for African missions. She gave her best toys to poor children. At school, she gave her snacks to poor classmates; when her mom packed extra snacks for her, she gave them all away. One day she took an apple from a neighbor's tree without asking. Her mother told her that though it would be embarrassing, she must return the apple and apologize. Chiara did. The neighbor gave Chiara a box of apples because she had learned something important that day.

When Chiara was nine, she joined the Focolare Movement, a Catholic organization devoted to worldwide unity in Christ. She also enjoyed tennis, hiking, swimming, singing, dancing, and spending long evenings with friends.

Chiara struggled with school and failed the first year of high school, but she persevered. When she was sixteen, she went on a Focolare retreat in Rome and developed a deep devotion to Jesus. While playing tennis, she felt pain in her shoulder. The pain continued and doctors found she had bone cancer. Chiara offered her pain to Jesus, praying, "It's for you, Jesus; if you want it, I want it too." She cheered other patients, her doctor, parents, and friends with her joyfulness. She gave all her money to a friend who was becoming a missionary to Africa. As she grew more ill, she told her mother not to be sad for her: "Don't shed any tears for me. I'm going to Jesus." She died in October 1990 before her 19th birthday.

Bl. Chiara Luce Badano ■

1971–1990

Feast Day:
October 29

Chiara was born in a small Italian village. In kindergarten, she started saving her money so she could give it to people who were going to help people in Africa. She gave her best toys to poor children. At school, she gave her snacks to poor classmates.

When Chiara was nine, she joined a Catholic group that brought Christians around the world together. She also enjoyed tennis, hiking, swimming, singing, dancing. School was hard for Chiara, but she kept trying. When Chiara was 16, she went on a retreat in Rome. She became even more devoted to Jesus.

One day she felt pain her shoulder while she was playing tennis. The pain continued and doctors told her she had cancer in her bones. Cancer is a deadly and painful disease that doctors cannot always fix.

Chiara offered her pain to Jesus. She prayed, "It's for you, Jesus; if you want it, I want it too." She cheered other patients, her doctor, parents, and friends with her joyfulness. She gave all her money to charity. As she grew more sick, she told her mother not to be sad for her. She died in October 1990. She was 18 years old.

St. Josemaría Escrivá

1902-1975

Feast Day:
June 26

Josemaría was born in a Spanish Catholic family. One winter day, he saw footprints of bare feet in the snow. A monk was walking in the snow to the church. Josemaría decided he wanted to suffer for God too and do whatever God wanted. He became a priest so that he could live always listening to God's call. Fr. Escrivá moved to Madrid, where he gathered university students and people of many professions to help him care for poor, sick people.

When he was twenty-six, he founded Opus Dei, an institution within the Church for evangelization. Opus Dei is a Latin phrase for "the work of God." Its first members were the university students he knew. Fr. Escrivá had to flee to survive persecution during the Spanish civil war. When the war ended, he traveled through Spain holding retreats for priests. He established the Priestly Society of the Holy Cross so that Opus Dei could include priests and lay people. Opus Dei spread to many countries, including Portugal, Italy, France, Ireland, Great Britain, Kenya, and the United States.

Fr. Escrivá moved to Rome to oversee the many projects of Opus Dei: elementary, secondary, and professional schools, universities, agricultural training centers, hospitals and clinics, and retreat centers. Fr. Escrivá helped in Vatican Council II. He journeyed through Europe and Latin America speaking to people about God's love, the sacraments, and the sanctity in daily work and family life. He was devoted to Our Lady. He hung a picture of her in all his rooms. He was sitting before a picture of her when he died.

St. Josemaría Escrivá

1902–1975

Feast Day:
June 26

Josemaría was born in a Spanish Catholic family. One winter day, he saw footprints of bare feet in the snow. He saw a monk walking in the snow to the church. Josemaría decided he wanted to suffer for God too and do whatever God wanted. He wanted to answer God's call every day, so he became a priest.

Fr. Escrivá moved to Madrid, the capital of Spain. There, he got people together to help him care for poor people and sick people. When he was 26, he founded a group called Opus Dei. Opus Dei means "the work of God." Its members work to share Jesus' love with others. The first members were students he knew.

Opus Dei spread to many countries throughout the world. Opus Dei projects include schools, hospitals, and retreat centers.

Fr. Escrivá journeyed through Europe and Latin America speaking about God's love. He told them they could be holy every day at school, with their families, and at work. He was devoted to Our Lady. He hung a picture of her in all his rooms. He was sitting before a picture of her when he died.

St. Maximilian Kolbe

1894-1941

Feast Day:
August 14

Raymund Kolbe was born in Poland. He entered a Franciscan monastery when he was 16. There he received the name Maximilian. He was ordained a priest in 1919. He taught men who were preparing to be priests and opened friaries (religious communities) in Poland, Japan, and India.

When he returned to Poland, the Nazis had invaded the country. Fr. Kolbe organized a shelter for thousands of Polish refugees. In 1941, the Nazis raided the shelter. They took Fr. Kolbe and his companions to Auschwitz, a Nazi death camp.

Fr. Kolbe was tortured and beaten by the Nazi guards. Though he was suffering, he offered to help the other prisoners. At night he would ask each one, "I am a Catholic priest. Can I do anything for you?" He would hear their confessions and tell them about God's love. He wouldn't ask for medical help until all his fellow prisoners had been treated.

One day a prisoner from the camp escaped. The guards announced that to prevent future escape attempts, 10 prisoners would be starved to death. The guards choose 10 men, including one young man who cried out in anguish for his wife and children. Fr. Kolbe stepped forward and volunteered to take the man's place. Fr. Kolbe was put in a cell with the other 9 men, where he prayed and read the Psalms with them. After two weeks of hunger and thirst, Fr. Kolbe was still alive. The Nazis injected poison into Fr. Kolbe's arm and he died.

The man Fr. Kolbe saved survived the war. At first that man felt regret. He felt like he had caused Fr. Kolbe's death by allowing himself to be saved. But then he understood: "A man like Fr. Kolbe could not have done otherwise. Perhaps he thought that as a priest his place was beside the condemned men to help them keep hope. In fact he was with them to the last."

St. Maximilian Kolbe

1894-1941

Feast Day:
August 14

Raymund Kolbe was born in Poland. He entered a Franciscan monastery when he was 16. There he received the name Maximilian. He was ordained a priest in 1919. He taught men who were preparing to be priests, and opened a religious community in Poland. He traveled to Japan and to India and opened communities there too.

When he returned to Poland, the Nazis had invaded the country. The Nazis were rounding up Jews and putting them in death camps. Fr. Kolbe organized a shelter for thousands of Polish people who had nowhere to go. In 1941, the Nazis raided the shelter. They took Fr. Kolbe and his companions to a death camp. Fr. Kolbe wrote a letter to his mother, telling her not to worry about him.

Life in the prison was very hard for Fr. Kolbe, but he always put the other prisoner's needs ahead of his own. The guards beat and tortured him. But he wouldn't ask for medical help until all his fellow prisoners had been treated. Though he was suffering, Fr. Kolbe helped the other prisoners. He would ask each one, "I am a Catholic priest. Can I do anything for you?" He heard their confessions. He told them about God's love.

One day a prisoner escaped. The guards said that 10 prisoners would be starved to death as a punishment. The guards choose 10 men. One of the men cried out in grief for his wife and children. Fr. Kolbe stepped forward and volunteered to take the man's place. Fr. Kolbe was put in a cell with the other 9 men. He prayed and read the Psalms with them. After two weeks of hunger and thirst, Fr. Kolbe was still alive. The Nazis injected poison into Fr. Kolbe's arm and he died.

The man Fr. Kolbe saved survived the war.

St. Thérèse of Lisieux

1873-1897

Feast Day:
October 1

Thérèse Martin was born in Alençon, France. Her mother and father had nine children, and Thérèse was one of five who survived. Thérèse's mother died when Thérèse was only 4 years old. Her father moved the family to Lisieux, and Thérèse's older sisters helped take care of her.

For much of her life, Thérèse was delicate and sensitive. She would cry if she thought someone was criticizing her. Then she would feel even worse about herself because she had cried.

Two of her sisters were nuns at a Discalced Carmelite convent. Thérèse also received a call to religious life, but she was too young to join the convent. But Thérèse did not give up. When she was 15, she went on a pilgrimage to Rome. Her group was able to visit the Pope, and she asked him for special permission to enter the convent. One of the Pope's officers saw her and was impressed with her courage. She was given permission to enter the convent. Thérèse would be a cloistered nun, meaning she would spend her days in prayer, away from other people and the world.

Thérèse knew that Jesus wanted the little ones to come to Him. In fact, Jesus Himself had become a child! So Thérèse was glad she was little. Thérèse also wanted to be holy. At first she felt discouraged when she compared herself to the saints. But instead of feeling discouraged, she persevered. She wrote: "In spite of my littleness, I can aim at being a saint. ... I will look for some means of going to heaven by a little way which is very short and very straight, a little way that is quite new." St. Thérèse is known for this "Little Way" of seeking holiness in ordinary, everyday things.

In 1896 she started coughing up blood. She had tuberculosis, which is a painful and deadly illness. She died less than a year later at age 24. The wisdom in her writings was so profound that Pope John Paul II named her a Doctor of the Church.

St. Thérèse of Lisieux

1873-1897

Feast Day:
October 1

Thérèse Martin was born in Alençon, France. Her mother died when she was only 4. She was a sensitive little girl. She would cry if people spoke to her harshly. Then she would feel even worse because she had cried.

Two of her sisters were nuns. Thérèse also received a call to religious life. She was too young to join the convent, but she did not give up. She even asked the Pope for special permission to enter the convent when she was in Rome. She was able to enter the convent. Thérèse spent her days in prayer, away from other people and the world.

Even as she grew older, Thérèse liked being little. She knew that Jesus wanted the little ones to come to Him. Jesus Himself had become a child! So Thérèse wanted to stay little. Thérèse also wanted to be holy. She wrote: "In in spite of my littleness, I can aim at being a saint." St. Thérèse is known for her idea of the "Little Way." The Little Way means seeking to show God's love in ordinary, everyday things.

In 1896 Thérèse became sick. She died less than a year later. She was only 24. St. Thérèse was little, but her writings and ideas about God's love were big. Pope John Paul II named her a Doctor of the Church.

St. Gianna Beretta Molla ■ ■

1922–1962

Feast Day:
April 28

Gianna was the tenth of thirteen children in a Catholic Italian family. When she was twenty, she went to Milan to study medicine. After graduating medical school, she opened an office. Her patients were children. One of her brothers was a missionary priest in Brazil. She wanted to join him and help care for the people there, but her own health problems kept her in Italy.

When she was 32, she met a man named Pietro Molla. A year later, Pietro and Gianna married; they had four children. While Gianna was pregnant with their fourth child, Gianna grew very sick. She had a tumor growing in her womb near her unborn baby.

Gianna was given three choices: she could have an abortion. She could ask the doctors to take out her womb. Or she could ask the doctors to take out only the tumor. Gianna refused to have an abortion, because it is a sin to kill an unborn baby on purpose. Gianna did not want the doctors to take out her womb because that would kill her baby too. Instead, Gianna asked the doctors to take out only the tumor. The doctors did. But Gianna was still sick. She told her family that if she became so sick that the doctors could save only her life or the baby's, she wanted the doctors to save her baby's life. Finally on Holy Saturday, her baby was born, a little girl. Gianna lived for one more week and then she died. She was 39 years old.

St. Gianna Beretta Molla

1922–1962

Feast Day:
April 28

Gianna was born into a Catholic Italian family. She had twelve siblings. When she was 20, she went to a city in Italy called Milan. She went there so she could go to school to become a doctor. When she graduated, she opened an office. Her patients were children.

When she was 33 she got married. She and her husband had four children. While Gianna was pregnant with their fourth child, Gianna grew very sick. Gianna had a tumor growing in her womb near her unborn daughter. A tumor is a growth of bad cells in the body. Some tumors are very serious, like Gianna's was. The tumor had to be removed.

Gianna had to decide what to do. Some of the ways the doctors would treat her would have killed her baby. Gianna did not want that to happen. She asked her doctors to take out the tumor, but protect her baby.

The doctors took out the tumor, but Gianna was still sick. She knew that her doctors might have to decide between saving her, or saving her baby. She told her family she wanted her doctors to save her baby if they had to choose. Finally her little girl was born. Gianna lived for one more week and then she died. She was 39 years old.

St. Monica

331–387

Feast Day:
August 27

Monica was born in Northern Africa to Christian parents shortly after Christianity was legalized. Her parents gave her in marriage to a pagan man, Patricius. Patricius frequently criticized Monica and lost his temper, but Monica loved him still. She asked God to help her husband abandon his sins. Patricius and Monica raised three children, Augustine, Navigius, and Perpetua. Augustine became deadly sick, and Monica asked that he be baptized. At first, Patricius agreed. But when Augustine grew healthier, Patricius denied Monica's request. Augustine left home to study law at the university in Carthage. He lived a wicked life there. Monica prayed patiently for him and for her husband. After nearly twenty years of marriage, her husband converted to Christianity and was baptized. He died one year later.

When Augustine came home from school, he told his mother his beliefs. His beliefs were heretical. Monica sent him away from the dinner table, and he left the house and went to Rome. Monica later saw a vision that made her want to reconcile with her son. So Monica went to Rome, but Augustine had gone to Milan. Monica joined him in Milan and introduced him to the bishop there, St. Ambrose. Under St. Ambrose's instruction, Monica learned to pray more simply and give what she had to the poor. Augustine converted to Christianity. Monica and Augustine lived happily together as Augustine prepared for baptism. He was baptized that Easter at age 33 by St. Ambrose. Monica told her son, "There was indeed one thing for which I wished ... and that was that I might see you a Catholic Christian before I died."

While Monica and Augustine were waiting for a boat back to Africa, Monica became ill with a fever and died.

331–387

Feast Day:
August 27

Monica was born in Northern Africa. Her parents gave her in marriage to a pagan man, Patricius. Monica loved Paticius even though he sometimes said mean things to her and lost his temper. Patricus and Monica had three children.

Monica was Christian, and she wanted her husband and children to be Christian too. She asked God to help her husband resist sin. She was patient and loving. After they had been married almost 20 years, her husband converted to Christianity and was baptized. He died one year later.

Monica's son Augustine went away to school. He started living a wicked life. She prayed for her son to believe in Jesus and be good. When Augustine went to Italy, Monica followed him. She introduced him to the bishop. They prayed for Augustine and taught him more about Jesus.

Monica learned to pray more simply. She gave what she had to the poor. She was grateful to God when Augustine converted to Christianity. Monica and Augustine were both happy. Monica told her son, "There was indeed one thing for which I wished … and that was that I might see you a Catholic Christian before I died."

St. Thomas More

1478-1535

Feast Day:
June 22

Thomas More was born in London. From an early age he was very bright and interested in subjects like logic, Latin, history, and music. He went to good schools, and impressed his teachers. One said he spoke Latin as easily as he spoke English! He became a successful lawyer, and gave lectures on St. Augustine. Many of his friends were scholars and writers. More was also a successful writer. His book *Utopia* was a story about a "perfect" society. Later authors borrowed that idea and the utopian genre (or type of literature) is still very popular. He considered religious life, but he discerned that it was not his calling. He continued the practice of law, and served in Parliament, England's lawmaking body. He got married and had four children before his wife died suddenly.

By the early 1500s, More had married again and was serving as an advisor to King Henry VIII. The Protestant Reformation was tearing Europe apart. But More remained faithful. King Henry VIII wanted to divorce his wife and he tried to use the Bible to say divorce was okay. But More knew that the King was wrong. King Henry VIII finally broke England away from the Catholic Church. More refused to swear allegiance to the King as head of the Church of England. He knew that, going back the Apostles, the Pope was the true head of the Church Jesus had founded. The King put him in prison and took away his property. While he was in prison he wrote letters to his family and essays about Jesus. When the King found out, he had his writing materials taken away. More was convicted of treason and beheaded in 1535. His last words were: "I die the good King's servant, but God's first."

St. Thomas More

1478-1535

Feast Day:
June 22

Thomas More was born in London. He went to good schools, and impressed his teachers. One of his teachers said he spoke Latin as easily as he spoke English!

More became a successful lawyer. He was also a great speaker and great writer. He served in Parliament, which makes laws for England. Later he became a helper to the King of England, King Henry VIII.

The king wanted to divorce his wife. He tried to use the Bible to say divorce was okay. But More knew that the king was wrong. The king decided to break England away from the Catholic Church and start his own church. The king told More he had to stop being Catholic and be loyal to him. More said no. The king put More in jail. He took away More's property. The king even took More's writing materials so he wouldn't be able to send letters to his family. Finally the king had More beheaded.

More's last words were: "I die the good King's servant, but God's first."

St. Paul

Died 67 A.D.

Feast Day:
June 29

Paul was a Jew, and a Roman citizen. For years, Paul persecuted Christians because he thought Christianity was false. He traveled to Damascus to persecute Christians, but a light shone from heaven and Paul fell to the ground. A voice said: "Why do you persecute me?" Paul asked, "Who are you?" The voice answered, "I am Jesus." Then Paul believed that Jesus is God. When Paul stood up, he could not see, so his friends led him to Damascus. God sent Ananias, a Christian man, to Paul; Ananias miraculously healed Paul's eyes and baptized him.

Immediately, Paul preached the Gospel to Jews and Gentiles, worked miracles in Jesus' name, and established Christian churches in many cities. Some Roman politicians who hated Christianity ordered Paul to be beaten and imprisoned. An earthquake shook the prison doors open. Paul, however, did not escape; he stayed and preached to the guard, and baptized him and his family.

Paul went to Jerusalem to preach, and some Jews took him to their court for preaching Christianity. Paul's case was brought to the local Roman court where the Jews falsely accused him. Paul, being a Roman citizen, appealed to Caesar. On his way to Rome, Paul preached to his guards and to the sailors. A storm brought the boat to an island, and Paul preached to the island natives. When he arrived in Rome, he preached to crowds of Jews while waiting for his trail before Caesar, who released him. Paul preached in many countries and returned to Rome, where he was accused and imprisoned again, and then beheaded. He wrote fourteen letters to the people he converted to Christianity, and these letters are in the Bible.

St. Paul

Died 67 A.D.

Feast Day:
June 29

Paul was a Jew and a Roman citizen who lived around the time of Jesus.

For years, Paul made trouble for Christians. He thought Christianity was false. He traveled to Damascus, a city in Syria, to go after Christians. On his way a light shone from heaven. Paul fell to the ground.

A voice said: "Why do you persecute me?"

Paul asked, "Who are you?"

The voice answered, "I am Jesus."

Then Paul believed that Jesus is God. When Paul stood up, he could not see. God sent Ananias, a Christian man, to Paul. Ananias miraculously healed Paul's eyes and baptized him.

Right away, Paul preached the Gospel to everyone. He worked miracles and started Christian churches in many cities. Some Romans who hated Christianity ordered Paul to be beaten and put in jail. An earthquake shook the prison doors open. But Paul did not try to escape. Instead he stayed and preached to the guard. He baptized the guard and his family.

Paul traveled to many different parts of the world. Everywhere he went, he preached the Gospel. When returned to Rome, he was accused and out in jail again. The Roman emperor had Paul beheaded.

Paul wrote fourteen letters to the people he converted to Christianity. These letters are in the Bible.

St. Pope John Paul II

1920–2005

Feast Day:
October 22

Karol Wojtyla was born in Poland. His father was an army lieutenant and his mother was a schoolteacher, and his dream was to be an actor. When Nazis invaded Poland, his college education and his acting came to an end. He worked to avoid being deported to Germany. When he was 22, he secretly entered seminary. After World War II, the seminary re-opened publicly. He was ordained a priest soon after. After further study in Rome and Poland, he was made Bishop of Krakow in the 1960s, a time when Poland was suffering from atheistic and Communist ideas. He participated in Vatican II and helped write many of its documents. When he was elected Pope, he chose the name John Paul II.

As a Polish pope, John Paul II inspired the Poles to form Solidarity, a trade union that regained rule of Poland from the Communist party. Pope John Paul II worked to convert England back to Catholicism. He allowed Anglican priests (who can marry) to keep their wives and families and become Catholic priests.

Pope John Paul II founded World Youth Day, when young Catholics from around the world gather in one city to meet the Pope, pray with him, listen to him, and attend Mass he offers for them. He wrote influential encyclicals such as *Evangelium Vitae*, which is about the value of human life. His lectures on the human person, purity, and marriage are together known as Theology of the Body. He died in April 2005. Thousands of people, including nearly a hundred political and religious leaders, attended his funeral.

St. Pope John Paul II

1920–2005

Feast Day:
October 22

Karol Wojtyla was born in Poland. When he was a young man, a lot of evil things were happening in Europe. The Nazis were sending Jews, Catholics, and many other people to camps. At the camps those people were tortured and killed. Karol secretly went into seminary (a school that prepares men to be priests). He was made a priest soon after World War II ended.

But even though the war had ended, people in Poland were suffering. They were not free under a communist government. Fr. Wojtkla was made Bishop of Krakow (Poland) in the 1960s. When he was elected Pope, he chose the name John Paul II. He helped people of Poland free themselves from the Communist party. Pope John Paul II also tried to help England come back to Catholicism.

Pope John Paul II founded World Youth Day. On World Youth Days, young Catholics from all over the world come together to be with the Pope and attend Mass he offers for them.

He wrote many important essays and books that helped people learn more about God. He died in April 2005. Thousands of people came to his funeral.

St. Peter

Died 64 A.D.

Feast Day:
June 29

Simon was a fisherman. His brother Andrew introduced him to Jesus, and Jesus called Simon and Andrew to be Apostles. When Jesus asked His Apostles who they thought He was, Simon answered that Jesus was the promised Messiah, the Son of God. Jesus answered Simon, "You are Peter; and upon this rock I will build my church." The word "Peter" means "rock," and Jesus built the Church on the foundation of the papacy, with Peter as the first pope. Jesus allowed Peter to see the Transfiguration and also to pray with Him before He was arrested to be crucified. When men came to arrest Jesus, Peter cut off a man's ear with his sword, but Jesus healed the man's ear.

Jesus warned Peter that he would deny Jesus. Peter promised he would not, but while Peter waited for Jesus outside the courthouse, people asked Peter if he knew Jesus. Peter lied and said he did not; then Peter remembered Jesus' prediction and left, weeping.

Jesus was crucified and rose from the dead, and came to Peter, saying to him, "Feed my sheep." After Jesus had ascended into Heaven and the Holy Spirit descended to the apostles, Peter was the first Apostle to preach and to work miracles in Jesus' name. Peter was imprisoned, but an angel freed him and he continued to preach to Jews and to Gentiles. With St. Paul's help, Peter led the first Church council in Jerusalem. He wrote two letters that are in the Bible. The Roman emperor condemned Peter to be crucified; Peter asked to be crucified upside down because he was not worthy to die as Jesus did. His relics are in St. Peter's Basilica in Rome.

St. Peter

Died 64 A.D.

Feast Day:
June 29

Simon was a fisherman who lived around the time of Jesus. His brother Andrew introduced him to Jesus. Jesus called Simon and Andrew to be Apostles. Jesus told Simon, "You are Peter; and upon this rock I will build my church."

Jesus warned Peter that he would deny Jesus. Peter promised he would not. While Peter waited for Jesus outside the courthouse, people asked Peter if he knew Jesus. Peter lied and said he did not know Him. Peter remembered what Jesus had told him and left, weeping.

Jesus was crucified and rose from the dead. He came to Peter saying to him, "Feed my sheep."

Peter was the first Apostle to preach and to work miracles in Jesus' name. Peter was put in jail, but an angel freed him. He continued to preach to everyone. With St. Paul's help, Peter led the first Church council in Jerusalem. He wrote two letters that are in the Bible.

The Roman Emperor ordered Peter to be crucified. But Peter asked to be crucified upside down. He said he was not worthy to die as Jesus did. His relics are in St. Peter's Basilica in Rome.

Bl. Miguel Pro Juárez

1891-1927

Feast Day:
November 23

Miguel was born in Guadeloupe, Mexico. His family was devoutly Catholic. Young Miguel enjoyed doodling and drawing cartoons, and he was very good at it! When his sister entered a convent, Miguel began to hear the Lord calling him to be a priest. He entered a Jesuit seminary. (A seminary is a school that prepares future priests.) He was there when people who hated Catholics began taking over Mexico. The seminary was forced to close. He and his classmates escaped to the United States. He continued his preparation, and was made a priest in Europe in 1925.

Back in Mexico, being Catholic was illegal. Churches had been forced to close. Priests had to hide. Even though it was dangerous, Fr. Pro wanted to return to Mexico. He got permission to go. He began helping people in secret. He would wear disguises to stay safe while he tended to people's needs. Sometimes he would dress as a beggar. When he went into rich neighborhoods to ask people to help the poor, he would dress as a businessman. He even dressed as a policeman to offer Holy Communion to prisoners.

Someone told the police what Fr. Pro was doing, and he was arrested. The government lied and said Fr. Pro had tried to kill the president of Mexico. Fr. Pro was sentenced to death for a crime he did not commit. He was sent to a firing squad. He forgave his executioners, and prayed out loud for God to forgive them. He stood before them with his arms stretched out at his sides. He held a rosary in one hand and a crucifix in the other. His last words were "Viva Cristo Rey," which means "Praise Christ the King!"

Bl. Miguel Pro Juárez

1891-1927

Feast Day:
November 23

Miguel was born in Guadeloupe, Mexico. His family was devoutly Catholic. Miguel was called to become a priest.

While he was preparing, the government in Mexico started making bad laws. It became illegal to be Catholic. Churches had to close. Many priests were killed. Miguel and his classmates escaped. He was made a priest in 1925.

Even though it was dangerous, Fr. Pro wanted to return to Mexico. He got permission to go. He began helping people in secret. He would wear disguises to stay safe. Sometimes he would dress as a beggar. Other times he dressed as a businessman. He even dressed as a policeman to give Holy Communion to people in prison.

Someone told the police what Fr. Pro was doing. He was arrested. The government lied and said Fr. Pro had tried to kill the president of Mexico. Even though he was innocent, Fr. Pro was sentenced to death. He forgave his executioners, and prayed out loud for God to forgive them. His last words were "Viva Cristo Rey," which means "Praise Christ the King!"

St. Stephen

Died 37 A.D.

Feast Day:
December 26

Stephen was a Jewish man who became one of the first Christians. He was full of wisdom and faith from the Holy Spirit. The disciples of Jesus ordained him a deacon. He had the task of taking care of widowed women who became Christian, and Stephen also worked miracles. Some Jewish men who hated Christianity tried to argue with Stephen, but they could not outsmart the wisdom he received from the Holy Spirit. They were so angry that they bribed other men to falsely accuse Stephen of telling wicked lies about the Old Testament prophet Moses.

On these false accusations, Stephen was brought to the Jewish court. Stephen defended himself by telling the story of Moses. Moses saved the Israelites from the pagan Egyptians. But the Israelites betrayed Moses and God by worshiping a pagan idol. Stephen told the Jewish men that like Moses, every Old Testament prophet was betrayed and persecuted by the Jews, although the prophets tried to tell the Jewish people about Jesus. When Jesus came, He was also betrayed, persecuted, and killed by Jewish people, including by the men who arrested Stephen.

Then the Jewish men were filled with rage because they did not want to hear the truth. Then Stephen looked up, and he saw heaven, with Jesus standing at the right of God the Father. Stephen told the men what he saw, but they refused to listen. They dragged him out of the city and stoned him. Just before he died, Stephen prayed that Jesus would be merciful to the men who were killing him. A martyr is someone who is killed for his or her religious faith. St. Stephen is the first martyr of the Church.

St. Stephen

Died 37 A.D.

Feast Day:
December 26

Stephen was a Jewish man who became one of the first Christians. He was full of wisdom and faith from the Holy Spirit. He took care of widowed women who became Christian. Stephen also worked miracles in Jesus' name.

Some Jewish men who hated Christianity tried to argue with Stephen. But they could not outsmart the wisdom he received from the Holy Spirit. They paid other men to lie and say that Stephen had said bad things about the Old Testament prophet Moses.

Stephen was brought to the Jewish court. Stephen defended himself by telling the story of Moses and other Old Testament prophets. Stephen said that the Ancient Jews had betrayed every Old Testament prophet, even though those prophets had tried to tell them about Jesus. Then when Jesus came, He was also betrayed and killed, including by the men who arrested Stephen.

The Jewish men were filled with rage. Then Stephen looked up. He saw Heaven. He saw Jesus standing at the right of God the Father. Stephen told the men what he saw, but they would not listen. They dragged him out of the city and threw stones at him until he died. Stephen prayed that Jesus would show mercy to his killers.

Bl. Teresa of Calcutta

1910–1997

Feast Day:
September 5

Agnes Gonxha Bojaxhiu was born in Skopje, Yugoslavia, (now Macedonia) to a devoutly Catholic family. Her father died suddenly when she was only 8 years old. When she was 18, she set out for a convent in Ireland. She would never see her mother again. When she arrived, very few people there understood her language. One sister remembered her as "very small, quiet, and shy." She received the name Teresa after St. Thérèse of Lisieux.

Her community sent her to India, where she taught high school history and geography for many years. She learned to speak the local languages. One day in 1946, Mother Teresa was on a train to a retreat in Darjeeling. On that train she received a call to found her own religious order, the Missionaries of Charity. She said, "I heard the call to give up all and follow Christ into the slums to serve him among the poorest of the poor." Mother Teresa helped throughout India. She taught children the alphabet by writing in the dirt. She visited the poor and the ill, asking what they needed and helping them. Pope Paul VI and St. Pope John Paul II praised her work. She helped lepers, orphans, AIDs patients, alcoholics, and many others. Her order opened houses in over 100 countries. She tried to bring help to China, but she wasn't able to.

Mother Teresa won the Nobel Peace Prize in 1979. In her acceptance speech, she urged people to protect unborn babies. She continued to help throughout the world even as her health got worse. She died in 1997.

Bl. Teresa of Calcutta

1910-1997

Feast Day:
September 5

Agnes Gonxha Bojaxhiu was born in Yugoslavia. Her family was devoutly Catholic. She went to a convent (a place where nuns live) in Ireland when she was 18. There she received the name Teresa. She was quiet and shy. Very few people there understood her language.

Her community sent her to India. There she was a school teacher for many years. She learned to speak the local languages.

One day in 1946, Mother Teresa was on a train. On that train she received a call to serve "the poorest of the poor." She started her own religious community to do this work.

Mother Teresa helped people throughout India. Even if they were extremely poor, or had very serious diseases, Mother Teresa showed them love. She helped people no one else would help.

Pope Paul VI and St. Pope John Paul II praised her work.

Women joined her communities in over 100 countries. She continued to help throughout the world even as her health got worse. She died in 1997.

Saintly Dinner Party

Directions: Answer the questions based on the activity completed in class.

My saint:_____

Write down the names of the saints you met today. In the "Notes" column, write 1-2 ways this saint used his or her gifts and talents to serve the Lord and others, and anything else you found interesting about him/her. Then answer the questions below.

My dinner companions: **Notes**

_____   _____

_____   _____

_____   _____

_____   _____

_____   _____

_____   _____

_____   _____

1. How did your saint use the gifts and talents he or she received from God to serve God and help others?
2. If you could meet your saint, what would you say to him/her? What questions would you ask?
3. On the back of this paper, write a prayer asking one of the saints you "met" today to pray for you in a special way.

Three Saint Stories

Directions: Read the stories and then complete the chart.

St. Dominic Savio

Dominic Savio was born in a small village in northern Italy, the first child of parents who were deeply in love with Christ. His parents, recognizing the gift God gave them, named him Dominic, meaning "belonging to God." By the time Dominic was four years old he could pray on his own, and his parents would often find him praying alone, in quiet places around the house. Dominic's father worked away from home, so during the day he would help his mother with cleaning and housework. He eagerly waited for his father to come home and would greet him with much excitement and love. Dominic never needed reminders to pray before meals or going to bed, and he would even become frustrated when having meals with guests if they would not pray together before eating.

Dominic went to church each morning to pray with his mother. They would often arrive at the church before it was unlocked for the day. Not wanting to waste the time he could be spending in conversation with the Lord, Dominic would kneel down outside the church – even in snow and mud- until they were able to enter. Dominic was excited to become an altar server when he turned five. He dearly loved Jesus in the Eucharist, and because of his great devotion and reverence for the Eucharist, he was given special permission

to receive his First Communion early. He had learned his catechism well and spent even more time reading other spiritual books to prepare himself for such a gift. He repeatedly said throughout his life that his First Communion was "the happiest and most wonderful day of my life." On his First Communion Day Dominic made four special promises which he wrote neatly in his little notebook. The four promises were:

1. I will go to confession often, and as frequently to Holy Communion as my confessor allows.
2. I wish to sanctify the Sundays and festivals in a special manner.
3. My friends shall be Jesus and Mary.
4. Death rather than sin.

Dominic went to elementary school in his village, where he made great progress by his hard work and cleverness. When he was old enough, he attended the county school which was three miles from his house. Since he was now ten, he was able to walk to and from school on his own. One hot sunny day, a farmer stopped him to ask if he was not tired from walking. Dominic quickly replied, "Nothing seems tiresome or painful when you are working for a Master who pays well." His friends invited him to go swimming often, but Dominic refused to go, and he told them it was a situation that would be easy to offend God, as his friends had behaved in a vulgar manner on other times that they had gone.

Dominic's teacher at school arranged for him to meet John Bosco, who became his mentor and teacher at an oratory in another small town in Italy. John Bosco, who himself would become a saint, said that Dominic was always eager to follow the school rules and work as diligently as he could. He never was unhappy or complained about listening to long talks and sermons, but would show his interest by asking questions to clarify his thinking. At his new school, Dominic was careful in choosing his friends and was always obedient to his teachers. Dominic's mother wrote a letter to John Bosco saying, "You have many good boys, but none can match the good heart and soul of Dominic Savio. I see him so often at prayer, staying in church after the others; every day he slips out of the playground to make a visit to the Blessed Sacrament. When he is in church he is like an angel living in paradise."

Not long after Dominic began school at the Oratory, he listened to a talk on sainthood. He became very moved by three points of the talk:

1. That it is God's will that each person should become a saint.
2. That it is easy to become a saint.
3. That there is a great reward waiting in heaven for those who try to become saints.

For the next few days he was quiet and worried about exactly how he would live a saintly life, as this was the greatest desire of his heart. John Bosco quickly comforted him by telling him to continue to be his cheerful self, to be faithful to his studies, to persevere in prayer, and not to shy away from playing games with his classmates and friends. It was also at this time that Dominic learned that his name meant "belonging to God," and he became ever more excited to set about becoming a saint.

To help himself grow in holiness, Dominic began doing small acts of penance to deny himself and make more room for loving the Lord. His teachers noticed that he was doing too much that might affect his health, such as sleeping only with a thin blanket in the winter, wearing a hair shirt under his normal clothes, and only eating bread and drinking water. John Bosco reminded him that the best penance would be to do all of his duties with perfection and in littleness and humility, seeking nothing for himself. He also told him that obedience would be the greatest sacrifice. From that time on, Dominic decided to live by the philosophy, "I can't do big things but I want everything to be for the glory of God." He committed himself to never complaining about food or the weather, suffered everything in great cheerfulness, and would keep his eyes from distractions of the world. Dominic even began a special prayer group at his school to spread devotion to our Holy Mother. When his classmates were suffering or experiencing difficulties, Dominic made it his quiet mission to talk with them and give them cheerful encouragement. At this time his own health was deteriorating very quickly, but he was sure to not let it keep him from giving himself to others; he even came back to the oratory after his doctors ordered that he spend time at home. Once he returned to the oratory, John Bosco spoke with him and helped him understand the importance of returning home to spend his last days with his family. Dominic dearly wanted to spend his last moments at the oratory, but willingly submitted to returning home. His friends did not know how serious his sickness was, as he did not let much of his suffering show. He bid them goodbye and traveled back to his hometown.

Upon arriving home, his health declined very quickly, but through it all Dominic stayed calm and courageous. He received the sacraments of the Holy Eucharist, Reconciliation, Anointing of the Sick, and even received the papal blessing days before his death. Dominic died peacefully at home in the presence of his family.

St. André Bessette

St. André Bessette was born into a poor family in Montreal, Canada. His parents had him baptized immediately after his birth because he was very weak. André's poor health would be a battle he would face for the rest of his life.

André's parents were very devout and had great faith in God. Prayer was important to them, and it would be important for André as well. He prayed often and would come away feeling a great peace and joy from being with God.

As a child, his faith was tested as he suffered the loss of his father at age 9. His mother died a few years later, yet he never wavered in doing good for others and deepening his prayer life. Following the death of his parents, he and his siblings went to live with relatives on their farm. He struggled with many of the chores he was asked to do, as his poor health made him very weak. He pleaded with God, through the intercession of St. Joseph, to help him know what it was that he was supposed to do with his life, as there had to be something out there at which he could be successful. He tried many things including working in a bakery, a shoe shop, and a factory, but he walked away from each job recognizing that they were too difficult and caused him to become even sicker.

Throughout all of the feelings of frustration and difficulty, André prayed evermore insistently for guidance. One day the pastor at André's parish, who had noticed André's great devotion, asked him if he ever thought God might be calling him to the priesthood or religious life. André was convinced he was not very smart and much too weak to be called. Father reassured him that he needn't worry about his weaknesses, but to just pray. Meanwhile, Father wrote a note to a nearby community of brothers and priests, telling them that he would be sending them "a saint." At first the community turned André away, telling him he was too weak and ill to join their community. The archbishop intervened for him and he was eventually allowed to stay.

From this point on André became known as Brother André and was given very small duties that did not seem very significant. However, Brother André used these small tasks as great opportunities to make himself little before the Lord and to serve God even in the smallest things. Brother

André grew in great devotion and prayer, especially to St. Joseph. As doorkeeper and messenger, he shared his deep joy with everyone who came to visit the brothers and greeted them with deep love and compassion. Many people began to visit just to share stories with him, some of them very sad and troubling. Brother André would always assure them of his prayers, but he also invited them to seek the intercession of his very special saint friend—St. Joseph. Through this, Brother André brought great peace and calm to many troubled souls who would later come back to tell him they had been cured of their illnesses or relieved of their difficult burden. They claimed their triumphs to be bold miracles attributed to his intercession, but Brother André would always redirect their excitement and gratitude, giving God the credit and the glory. He often went to visit the sick in their homes and would entrust them to St. Joseph in prayer. More and more healings were attributed to the power of his prayers, yet he always refused to take any credit for them, instead giving St. Joseph the honor. Word spread quickly and even greater crowds of people came to the door to witness the humility and great trust Brother André had in the Lord. Throughout his long life, Brother André was scrutinized and seen as a crazy man by many, but he persevered in his sufferings, continuing to spread deep faith and devotion to prayer.

St. Rose Philippine Duchesne

Rose Philippine Duchesne was born in a large family in France. She lived with her immediate family as well as her aunt,

uncle, and cousins. Between the two families there were 20 children in all, so Rose was never without excitement and opportunities to help others. She learned from her mother at a very young age to put others before herself, and she always tried to follow her mother's example. At church she loved to listen to the missionary priests from America tell stories of their work with the Native Americans.

Rose and her siblings were homeschooled until she reached the age of 12, when she was sent with her cousin to be educated in a monastery known for its prestige. The monastery was located near a community of Visitation Sisters who helped with the teaching. Rose loved learning from the sisters about the lives of the saints and their impact on history, and she was intrigued by the peaceful and prayerful lives of the sisters who taught her. She prayed fervently that God would show her how she could love and serve Him best.

When her father found out about her ever-growing attraction to the life of the sisters, he pulled her from the school and had her tutored at home with the rest of her siblings and cousins. A short while later, when Rose was eighteen, she made the decision to enter the Visitation Sister's community, despite her family's disapproval.

A few years later, however, persecution of Catholics began, and French Revolutionaries forced the sisters to shut down the monastery and disperse throughout the country. Rose went home to live with her family. For ten years, Rose lived at home and continued to live a life dedicated to serving God and others. She visited and cared for the sick, as well as educated young children.

When the war was over Rose wanted to go back to the convent, and she prayed to see what God had in store for her. She and a few of her sisters returned to the monastery and found everything in shambles. They attempted to repair and rebuild the community, but were not successful. Rose, meanwhile, heard about a new community being formed in northern France. She became a very dear friend of Mother Barat, the Superior of the community, and the two communities merged into one. Rose now became Sister Philippine.

In one of her conversations with Mother Barat, Sister Philippine told her of her lifelong desire to be a missionary in America. She told her she wanted to serve the Native Americans and those who were less fortunate. Instead, Mother Barat sent Sister Philippine to Paris, the capital of France, to work with the poor. Sister never gave up her dream of going to America, however. One day her prayers were finally answered when Mother Barat told her that an American bishop had asked for help in America. Sister Philippine could not contain her excitement! She and four other sisters sailed to America on a long and difficult 10-week journey.

When they finally arrived in Louisiana, the sisters found out that the bishop had not arranged any housing for them. They eventually traveled up the Mississippi River and settled in St. Charles, Missouri. They quickly built a log cabin and opened a school. They endured many difficulties in settling in a remote area. It was hard to find food and fresh water. The summers were very hot, and the winters were bitter cold. Mother Philippine Duchesne, as they now called her, never gave up and was never heard complaining about the conditions. She was dedicated to the service of the poor in the area. All the while that she taught, cooked, cleaned, gathered wood, and made clothing, her prayer never ceased. The sisters continued to open schools and build additional convents, but Mother Duchesne's desire to work with the Native Americans was still stirring deep in her heart.

When she was seventy-one, Mother Duchesne's dream finally came true: she had received an invitation to work with the Native Americans in Kansas! However, the difficulties did not stop. When she arrived in Kansas, Mother Duchesne was not able to successfully learn the Native American language. Instead of going home in defeat, she spent many hours in prayer for the people she was sent to help. The children of the community began to call her the "Woman Who Prays Always," and she had a big influence on them even without words.

When her health began to decline, Mother Duchesne decided to return to Missouri. Her life was very lonely, and she suffered much for the souls of the people the sisters served. Never giving up her faith despite her struggles, she often said, "He who has Jesus, has everything."

Saint	What special talents did this saint have?	How did she/he use these talents to serve God and others?	What was your favorite part of this saint's story?

Answer Key

Sacred Art and Catechesis

1. Accept reasoned answers.

2. An icon is a flat painting, usually on wood, of Our Lord, Our Lady, or a saint(s).

3. Like all good art, icons can help us connect spiritually to the saints by helping focus our minds and imaginations.

4. Icons have a religious focus, and tend to be very simple. Where art in modern contexts often tends to be bright, busy, constantly changing, and so forth, icons facilitate stillness and silent contemplation. Focusing on them can help us quiet our minds enough to be able to hear God speaking to us.

5. Accept reasoned answers.

6. To focus our minds on the Lord and examples of holiness, to aid us in intercessory prayer. At home, the use of icons and other sacred art can extend Catholic beliefs and devotions into every room of the house.

7. The collage is a sign of how rich and varied the call to holiness is among the members of the Church.

Rejoice and Be Glad:
The Poem of the Beatitudes

by Sean Fitzpatrick, Headmaster, Gregory the Great Academy

"Blessed are the − a − a − "

"Poor" −

"Yes − poor; blessed are the poor − a − a − "

"In spirit − "

"In spirit; blessed are the poor in spirit, for they − they − "

"Theirs − "

"For theirs. Blessed are the poor in spirit, for theirs is the kingdom of heaven. Blessed are they that mourn, for they − they"

"Sh − "

"For they − a − "

"S, H, A − "

"For they S, H − Oh, I don't know what it is!"

"Shall!"

"Oh, shall! for they shall − for they shall − a − a − shall mourn − a − a − blessed are they that shall − they that − a − they that shall mourn, for they shall − a − shall what? Why don't you tell me, Mary? − what do you want to be so mean for?"

There is reason to open a reflection on the Beatitudes with an excerpt from Tom Sawyer's Sunday schooldays rather than an excerpt from a Sunday sermon by Augustine, Chrysostom, Ambrose, Gregory, or Leo. The Beatitudes belong in the mouths of babes and sucklings before running a course in the minds of bishops and saints. Christians merit beatitude only because they answer the command to become childlike in trust and cheer. For this reason, the Beatitudes emphasize happiness together with holiness. Every child should have a catalogue of reassuring poetical principles that are held by heart. Every child is motherless without Mother Goose − and fatherless without Our Father; and for those who would become as little children, the Beatitudes can assume the ringing, singing solidity of the nursery. The Beatitudes are not rigid laws, but attitudes of virtue and blessedness that bring joy. Like nursery rhymes, they frame the truths of reality, the human condition, and the divine plan; informing young hearts − and the young at heart − on the ways and wonders of the world and providing the happiness that leads on to heaven.

Despite Tom Sawyer's perfectly poor performance, the Beatitudes are in no way wasted on children. Their wisdom is for children − and the childlike − to keep in their hearts' pockets as little keys to the Kingdom. The greatest secrets of the world are not to be withheld from the little ones. "The gates of heaven are lightly locked," says Our Lady in Chesterton's glorious ballad. Therefore, every child's Penny Catechism lays out the summation of existence on the first page: God made man to know, love, and serve Him in this world and to be happy with Him in the next. Or, *The world is so full of a number of things, I'm sure we should all be as happy as kings*, to rephrase this doctrine of the Garden of Eden in the dialect of the Garden of Verses.

The Beatitudes are the code of human happiness; and happiness is nothing to be suspect of, for "happiness," as St. Thomas Aquinas declares, "is the end of life," and the Beatitudes are the path. There is no such thing as a sad saint. Happiness is essential to holiness, and the example of children, who are famed and celebrated as happy, is central to the paradoxical blessedness of the Beatitudes: rejoicing in things invisible and imparting an earthly taste of the heavenly happiness that is to come, and a taste for it as well. Happiness is bestowed to the poor in spirit, the meek, the merciful, the clean of heart, the peacemakers – a gift given and received as a parent to a child.

The happiness of the Beatitudes lies in a type of virtue that is built upon simplicity, humility, and felicity. Man must be master of his action, as Aristotle taught, but he must also remember to be a child as well as a chief. An act of true, religious virtue is not only one of habit, freedom, and self-determination, but also one of worship. Love is central, which renders virtue more of a state of being rather than doing, of living in love, and the happiness that is given as the resulting gift. This is Christian

virtue – the virtue that requires both the independent, determined strength of manhood and the dependent, loving heart of childhood – and it is the outlook of the Beatitudes. It is the difficult balance between the dove and the serpent: the simplicity and strength that aligns human will to God's will. It is difficult to grow into maturity; it is even more difficult to be reborn as a little child, learning to see things again for the first time and to receive life from God rather than realizing it independently.

The Beatitudes are verses in the song of creation, being the promises of happiness to those who faithfully, lovingly, and worshipfully accept Christ's teachings and His divine example. They are the refrains of the New Covenant where happiness is assured on earth as it is in heaven. They afford not merely a renewed vision, but a new vision in which time and eternity meet; where the pagan lament for the "tears in things" is elevated into a hymn of everlasting joy. Though there is, of course, inescapable loss in life, there is also a sense in which things do not change or even diminish – in the heart of God, and the eyes of a child, all things are made new.

This reality, this mystery, is the element of nursery rhymes, which serves as a measure and mantra of the wide world and the happiness it holds. As these poems settle comfortably into the hearts of children, structuring their worldview, so should the Beatitudes act on the children of Christ as rejoicing and glad tenets that show the Way to St. Ives and the rest of the company of saints, providing perspective on the justice of God and the happiness that is the end of life. Even those who mourn and suffer will live happily ever after, as is reinforced by the lore and limericks of the nursery.

As such, the Beatitudes, like any of the old optimistic rhymes, belong in the everyday songs of all Christians, old and young alike, for their actuality and applicability expands, extends, and adapts over time. The Beatitudes are truly poetic, for they are impenetrable and beautiful expressions of experience. Poetry, like any profundity, is concentrated thought; and though a poem may never be fully understood, its meaning is slowly revealed throughout life. A poem is learned and loved more and more as life advances.

This truth is especially true regarding the Beatitudes. These teachings take a lifetime to learn for they are about life itself and the perfection of the specifically Christian life. Each of the eight has a meaning that is like a seed, which, planted in a wondering mind, grows eventually into a tree of complexity, strength, beauty, and wisdom. And so should all, following at least part of the example of Tom Sawyer, apply these words of the mount to heart and mind alongside Jack and Jill of the hill.

Blessed are the poor in spirit; for theirs is the kingdom of heaven

Those who humble themselves freely are promised glory for they begin their blessedness at the beginning – uprooting pride, which is the root of evil. The poor in spirit are the humble ones, whose humility is the foundation upon which all other virtues may be built up as a solid stronghold. The proud have not such a base, whose high spirit is like a shifting wind that puffs and blows. The poor in spirit have not such blustering spirits. They are humble in faith and in self-knowledge, going through life like jolly beggars ever in need of God's help, and resting secure in the promise of the riches of heaven.

Blessed are the meek; for they shall possess the land

Meekness is not weakness – it is strength. Though the meek do not resist evil with force, they overcome it with patient and enduring goodness. The meek are those whose reason guides impulse, restraining anger and passion. They are not free from anger or without passions, but have the will to control and master them. In this lies their strength, their virtue. In short, the meek possess themselves; and therefore, shall be rewarded with the possessions of the King of kings.

Blessed are they that mourn; for they shall be comforted

Mourning is different from sadness, for it is sadness coupled with sense. It is less impassioned. It is attentive and reflective. Though people mourn their dead, this celestial promise is beyond the funereal. Comforting those who mourn the death nature doles is natural. Comforting those who mourn the death sin doles is supernatural. Mourners over the shortcomings of mankind will not be left to the death of despair, says the Lord. Comfort will come in the form of pardon and peace, which is the end of all sorrow and the entering into the comforts which are consolations here for they presage the hereafter.

Blessed are they that hunger and thirst after justice; for they shall have their fill.

It is not enough to dream of justice. It is not enough to wish for justice. Justice must be hungered after and thirsted after as a means – as a requisite – of wellbeing and existence. Moreover, just as hunger and thirst can never be forever satiated in this life, neither can the need for the divine gifts of justice. This longing, which is the longing of the saints, will know satisfaction, but only complete satisfaction in the bounty of heaven.

Blessed are the merciful; for they shall obtain mercy

The merciful are those who make others' miseries their own, strive to relieve them, and thus are themselves spared from misery. The benevolence of humanity is so pleasing to Divinity that it is rewarded with God's own benevolence, which surpasses all earthly mercy to realms of happiness and blessedness that are inexpressible. It is His mercy that seasons justice, as it does in the mightiest, in a balance of happiness.

Blessed are the clean of heart; for they shall see God

Those who have washed themselves of sin and stain in virtue's running stream are fit to be brought before the countenance of God – both in this life, as though through a glass darkly, and in the next, as a resplendent beatific vision. It is with the eyes of the heart that the most essential is seen, and to the heart that is pure, this sight is granted. The heart is also understood as the Temple of God, and God will only reside in those hearts, those temples, which are well prepared for His presence. Without the inward eyes of the heart, the outward eyes are blind to the invisible realities; for though many partake at the king's table, only those of clean heart can behold Him face to face at the same time.

Blessed are the peacemakers; for they shall be called the children of God

Peace is the child of order. Order is the child of harmony between the related and unrelated, giving all things right relation to each other with rejoicing. The maker of peaceful rejoicing is the child of God. When those who have first made peace within their own hearts share this order with their anxious or agitated brethren, this inheritance comes into play. These are not only makers of peace, but also lovers of peace, having it enthroned in the heart and not merely enacted in the body. Those who love peace are children of the Prince of Peace, for as Christ came to gather and harmonize, so should His children be perpetrators of that holy mission, resembling their Father.

Blessed are they who are persecuted for the sake of righteousness; for theirs is the kingdom of heaven

Many are the ways to be a martyr because many are the ways of persecuting. What is important, however, is not the form or

La Madonna di San Sisto (detail), Raphael

source of persecution, but the martyrdom. It is not important who or what persecutes, but why. To those who suffer persecution for the justice of God and His Only Begotten Son, Who is Justice Himself, a kingdom is laid up. Like the poor in spirit, those put down are destined to rise because, together, they scorn the wiles and wickedness of the world.

Blessed are you when they insult you and persecute you and utter every kind of evil against you falsely because of me. Rejoice and be glad, for your reward will be great in heaven. (Matthew 5:11-12)

It is one thing to be accused of evil or evilly insulted in person. It is another to be abused in absence. To have one's good name reviled without knowledge or chance to react is a deep injury and craven persecution. Even this, however, can be a blessing if they are suffered for the right reasons. No Christian should glory in their persecution or in wicked words driven against them, but offer these to the greater glory of God, for in this only is gladness and rejoicing. This is the foretaste of the promised reward, a rejoicing in spiritual things now and to come – which gladness will be perfected in the kingdom of heaven.

The Beatitudes are the victorious pronouncement of virtues that require a childlike virtuosity. This playful mastery can come to beauteous and bounteous fruition by including and incorporating the Beatitudes in the same way that "Little Boy Blue" is included and incorporated in general consciousness. Let the words of Christ on the Mount be written on the heart (hopefully with more precision than Tom Sawyer) and there let them lie. Let them speak and sing as life is lived and loved, and as the God Who is Life and Love turns the fiery cosmos where His happiness can be had before it is held by the blessed.

Questions for Discussion

1. In what way are the Beatitudes like children's rhymes?

2. What does it mean for Christians to be grownup and childlike at the same time? Why is this idea paradoxical? (Compare the images of the serpent and the dove.)

3. How are the Beatitudes paradoxical? How is that paradox consistent with Christianity?

4. Why should people young and old learn the Beatitudes by heart?

5. How do the Beatitudes apply themselves to current situations that Christians face?

6. Why do the Beatitudes grant happiness on earth as well as in heaven?

7. Recite a poem you learned as a child. Why should you be able to recite the Beatitudes in the same way?

High School Lesson Connections to USCCB Framework

Our Eternal End Is Heaven

Life in Jesus Christ:
    I. A. 1. a–c
    I. A. 2. a, b
    II.A. 1-3
    V.A.1-3
    V.B.1
    V. C. 3

Revelation of Jesus Christ in Scripture:
    I.B.1.e.

Conscience: God's Voice in Our Hearts

Life in Jesus Christ:
    II. C. 3, 5
    III. F. 1, 3, 4
    V. A. 1-3
    V. C. 3
    V. D. 1

Vocation: The Universal Call to Holiness

Life in Jesus Christ:
    III. A
    III. B. 1. b. 1-3

Responding to the Call of Jesus Christ:
    I. A. 1, 2, 4
    I. B. 4
    IV. A. 2
    V. B.

The Passions in the Christian Life

Life in Jesus Christ:
    I. B. 3. c
    II. C. 3, 5

The Reality of Sin and the Necessity of Virtue

The Mission of Jesus Christ:
    I. A. 3. a-c
    II. A. 1

Life in Jesus Christ:
    III. D. 1, 2. a–b
    IV. C. 2
    IV. D
    V. B. 1, 4, 6
    V. D. 4-5

Obedience

Who Is Jesus Christ?
    II. D. 5. a

The Mission of Jesus Christ:
    I. A. 3. a-c

Life in Jesus Christ:
    V. A. 1-3
    V. C. 4

The Beatitudes and Moral Choices

Life in Jesus Christ:
    II. B. 1-2, a-c
    II. C. 3, 5
    V. D. 4

Who Are the Blessed?

Life in Jesus Christ:
> I. A. 1. a-c; 2. a, b
> I. B. 1
> I. B. 2. a-c
> I. B. 3. a-c
> II. B. 2. c. 1. a-h
> II. C. 3

Beatitudes and the Saints

Jesus Christ's Mission Continues in the Church:
> III. B. 6

History of the Catholic Church
> II. 1. B. 2. b
> II. 4, B. 9
> II. 6. A. 1
> II. 6. B. 2-3
> II. 7. E. 3
> II. 9. C. 3
> II. 16. A

Rejoice and Be Glad:
The Poem of the Beatitudes

Life in Jesus Christ:
> II. B. 2. c. 1. a-h